This Is Mouse

An ADVENTURE in Sewing

Make Mouse & Friends
Travel with Them from Africa to Outer Space

Brenna Maloney

FunStitch
STUDIO

stitch your art out.

Text copyright © 2014 by Brenna Maloney

Photography copyright © Chuck Kennedy

Artwork copyright © 2014 by C&T Publishing, Inc.

Publisher: Amy Marson

Creative Director: Gailen Runge

Art Director: Kristy Zacharias

Editor: Lynn Koolish

Technical Editors: Debbie Rodgers and Teresa Stroin

Cover Designer: April Mostek

Book Designer: Kristen Yenche

Production Coordinator: Rue Flaherty

Production Editor: Katie Van Amburg

Illustrator: Tim Manibusan

Photography by Chuck Kennedy

Published by FunStitch Studio, an imprint of C&T Publishing, Inc.,
P.O. Box 1456, Lafayette, CA 94549

Attention Teachers: C&T Publishing, Inc., encourages you to use this book as a text for teaching. Contact us at 800-284-1114 or ctpub.com for lesson plans and information about the C&T Creative Troupe.

We take great care to ensure that the information included in our products is accurate and presented in good faith, but no warranty is provided nor are results guaranteed. Having no control over the choices of materials or procedures used, neither the author nor C&T Publishing, Inc., shall have any liability to any person or entity with respect to any loss or damage caused directly or indirectly by the information contained in this book. For your convenience, we post an up-to-date listing of corrections on our website (ctpub.com). If a correction is not already noted, please contact our customer service department at ctinfo@ctpub.com or at P.O. Box 1456, Lafayette, CA 94549.

Trademark (™) and registered trademark (®) names are used throughout this book. Rather than use the symbols with every occurrence of a trademark or registered trademark name, we are using the names only in the editorial fashion and to the benefit of the owner, with no intention of infringement.

Library of Congress Cataloging-in-Publication Data

Maloney, Brenna.

This is Mouse : an adventure in sewing : make Mouse & friends--travel with them from Africa to outer space / Brenna Maloney.

     pages cm

Audience: Age 10 and up.

ISBN 978-1-60705-977-6 (soft cover)

1. Sewing--Juvenile literature. 2. Travel--Juvenile literature. I. Title.

TT712.M35 2014

646.2--dc23

                                    2014017513

Printed in China

10 9 8 7 6 5 4 3 2 1

Dedication

I dedicate this book to my husband. It's such a long road, isn't it?
But we make quite a team, you and I.

Acknowledgments

I'd like to thank my publisher—C&T Publishing—for allowing me to write the books I always wanted to read. Thanks also to my sons for their inspiration and support.

Contents

Meet Mouse

This is Mouse.

Mouse is soft with small, pink ears.

Mouse is easy to make.

You can make a Mouse just like this.

Mouse can be a boy or a girl. You can use any fabric you like. Mouse can have fancy clothes or run around naked. You can leave off the whiskers. Put on a funny hat. It's all up to you.

Once you get started, the possibilities are endless.

No matter what Mouse looks like, Mouse always likes to go on adventures. In this book, Mouse will go on three adventures. Mouse will go on a jungle safari, explore the South Pole, and blast off into space.

You can go on these adventures, too. But first you need to do a little sewing. Don't worry! It's not hard. I will show you how. Let's get started!

URGENT! VITAL! SUPER IMPORTANT!

Well, that might be overselling things a tad. What follows is not really urgent, vital, or terribly important. But before you make your Mouse, my editors wanted me to go over some ground rules. I'm not very good at ground rules, but my editors pointed out that this might be your first sewing book. Or you may just need a refresher course. It might be helpful, they said, if I went over a few key items. So, if you are not feeling equipped, read on. If you're good to go, skip to Making Mouse (page 15).

This Is Mouse—An Adventure in Sewing

Sewing Basics

WORDS TO KNOW

My editors tell me that it's very important that I teach you the proper words for things. As I am notorious for never using the proper words for anything, creating a glossary was something of a challenge for me. But I tried to do my best. Here are some useful terms that you may need to know as you make your way through this book.

Boogered: When something is boogered, it's all messed up. You sewed it backward or upside down or totally sideways. We all booger things up. I do it all the time. If something gets boogered, you might have to use a seam ripper (page 9) to uh … well … unbooger it.

Fat quarter: A fat quarter is a piece of fabric that is 18″ × 22″ (45.7cm × 55.9cm). Fat quarters are often found in quilt shops. A "regular" quarter of a yard of fabric is 9″ × about 44″ (22.9cm × 101.6cm).

Raw edge: The unfinished, cut edge of fabric.

Right side: There's a right side and a wrong side to fabric, and I'm not being judgmental here. The right side, or the front side, of the fabric has the design on it. I'll often ask you to sew "with right sides together." That means I want the two pieces of fabric facing each other.

Seam: This is an easy one. A seam is the line of stitching that joins two pieces of fabric.

Seam allowance: No, no, not the weekly sum of money that is doled out for doing chores. A seam allowance is the amount of fabric between the line of stitching and the edge of the fabric. Try to maintain a ¼″ (0.6cm) seam allowance for most of the projects in this book.

Turning: I don't mean turning *into* anything, like a werewolf or a vampire. In this book, *turning* refers to when you have something that's inside out and you need to make it right side out. You turn it, usually by way of a small gap that you left when you sewed it.

TOOLS OF THE TRADE

Marking pens: This book has a lot of patterns for you to follow when you sew. If you want to use the patterns in this book—as opposed to eyeballing the patterns in this book and then doing your own thing (which is perfectly acceptable)—you'll need a pen to mark them with. A lot of fabric stores sell pens made especially for this type of work. They aren't permanent; a lot of them wash off with water. I'll be honest when I tell you I'm not as careful when marking my patterns, and I sometimes use a black marker or even—gasp!—a Sharpie! And everyone knows that Sharpies are permanent and they can bleed through fabric. So, you might not want to follow my lead on that one. I've also been known to use ye ol' gel pen, especially if I'm working with a dark fabric.

Scissors: They work so much better than your teeth. Don't think that I don't know that you sometimes use your teeth to cut or tear, but listen: while that may work for cutting a thread, it's not going to work when you're cutting fabric. Just the image of you gnawing your way through a hunk of wool is, frankly, a little disturbing. So, please, use scissors. I often use a big pair for big jobs and a small pair for small jobs. Your orthodontist will thank you.

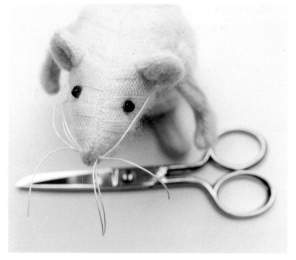

Pins: Good for holding together bits of fabric before sewing them. Do not carry them around in your teeth when you are not using them for Holding Bits of Fabric Before Sewing, okay? Every time I do this, I forget that they are there and then when I try to speak, I spray the listener with a volley of pins. Not cool. Use a pincushion. Or a box. Or something. Anything. Really.

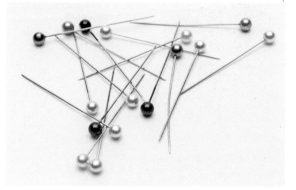

Thread: You'll need it. It's tough to sew anything without it. You may begin to wonder as you make your way through this book if I am, in fact, color blind. You will wonder this because I often use shockingly colored thread that no one in their right mind would ever use on purpose. It would be fair for you to wonder this, but let me tell you—there's a method to my madness. I use contrasting thread on most of the projects so that you can see what I'm doing. In most cases, you should not follow suit. You should use a matching thread—one that matches the color of your fabric—so that it cannot be readily seen.

Seam ripper: I'm not saying *you* will need to use one of these. You might be one of those flawless sewists who never sews things on backward. Me, I keep this baby handy because I'm always boogering things up.

Pokers: When turning (page 8), you may need to get an assist from something pointy (but not too sharp!). I use all sorts of things as pokers—pencils are good; chopsticks also work well.

Stuffing: As many of these projects are stuffed animals, you will need to stuff them. With something. Polyfill (a polyester stuffing) works well most of the time. On occasion, I might advise you to use rice. Rice can help you change the shape of an animal after you've made it and will give it added character. You can also use polyfill for most of your animal, then add a small amount of rice at the bottom to help it stand up straight. This works well for Mouse and Penguin.

Embellishments: That's code for "weird stuff." Embellishments can be simple things, like using beads or buttons for an animal's eyes. Or it can be odd stuff, like using sticks or sugar cubes to complete some of these projects. Be ready for anything, my friend, because I'm gonna throw some weird stuff at you.

Hot glue gun: My nemesis. You know this word, right? *Nemesis*? It literally means "a source of harm or ruin." And that's what the hot glue gun is for me. I know I need to use it. I know it will help me make stuff. But dang if I don't run the risk of singeing my digits off every time I pick the thing up. Am I unnaturally clumsy? Entirely possible. Will you fare much better than I when using this dastardly device? Hopefully. But do be careful. If you don't feel confident about using one, ask for help. Don't ask *me*, of course, because I'll just make a mess of it.

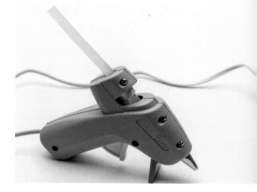

STITCHES TO KNOW

Backstitch: Okay. Not at all the same as *back talk*. Back talk is what you should *never* do to your parents. *Backstitch* is something I'll remind you to do from time to time to secure the stitching line so your sewing doesn't come unraveled. You start to sew a seam, stop, hold down the reverse button on your sewing machine, and sew a few stitches backward. Then stop, let go of the reverse button, and sew forward again. You should backstitch at the beginning and end of each seam.

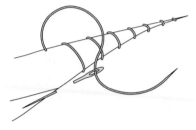

Ladder stitch: This is used to join two folded edges of fabric. Stitches are made at right angles to the fabric, creating a ladder-like formation between the fabrics, which are tightened and become invisible. Sounds like magic, no?

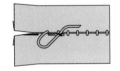

Slipstitch: A favorite of mine—used to join two folded edges or one folded edge to a flat surface, for an almost invisible stitch.

Straight stitch: As in, not zigzaggy. This is the most basic machine stitch. It makes a single row of straight, even stitches.

〰〰

Zigzag stitch: Zzzzzzzzzzzzzzzs. This Z-shaped machine stitch is another common stitch you can use for some of the patterns in this book.

TECHNIQUES

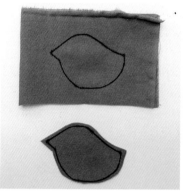

Sewing

Have you used a sewing machine before? If not, read your sewing machine manual or ask for help from a parent or other adult.

If you don't have a sewing machine, you can make all the projects by hand—it'll just take you a bit longer.

I don't really do anything fancy in this book. I use my trusty Kenmore sewing machine to do most of the sewing. And I use the most basic straight stitch it has to offer. Oh, sometimes I might go wild and use the zigzag stitch, but that's only when I'm feeling really crazy.

I do sew some pieces by hand, and I usually tell you when that might be a good idea to try. And I also sew by hand to close up the small gaps I left for turning an animal. You can use any stitch you like to do that—slipstitch or ladder stitch. When I'm attaching limbs to an animal by hand, I usually turn the raw edges under and use a slipstitch to attach it.

You remember what all these words mean, right? If not, go back to Words to Know (page 7), Tools of the Trade (page 8), and Stitches to Know (page 11) and refresh your memory. You can do this at any point in the book; they'll still be there.

For some of the projects in this book, you'll need to use pattern pieces, which I've supplied. There will be times when I tell you to cut out your pieces first, before you sew. And there will be other times when I'll tell you to mark around your patterns and then *sew two pieces together, before you cut* anything.

Curve Madness

Here's a bit to warn you about—a few of the patterns in this book (Penguin and Whale, to name a couple) will require you to sew together some curved pieces.

When you get to these points, I know you'll think I was dizzy when I wrote the instructions. You'll think to yourself, "Self … is Brenna an idiot? Why has she told me to sew these pieces together when they so obviously do not go together?!"

And at that point, you might say or think Bad Words and you might even be tempted to throw this book at a wall or, worse, grind it up in your garbage disposal. I do not recommend the garbage disposal route because it can be very damaging to the garbage disposal. And I'm not just saying that to try to protect my book. No, when you get to these places where you need to sew some curves, try to show *patience* and *restraint*. I am terrible at both patience and restraint, so what I do in these situations is line the fabric up (in the nonsensical way I have suggested), sew very slowly, and pull.

 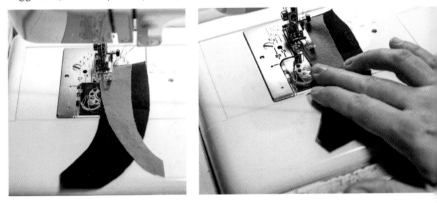

Yep, I gently tug on the fabric to get it to line up. When you're done sewing, the fabric will buckle like crazy and you'll think you've boogered it.

But once you iron it flat, you will see. It was all according to my evil plan (cue evil laugh).

Clipping Curves

Here's another odd thing I'll ask you to try. After you've sewn something with a curve, I'll ask you to make little cuts in the seam allowance. *Snip, snip, snippity snip.* It looks a bit like fringe now, doesn't it? It's not that I'm wanting you to embellish your seam allowance, exactly.

But by doing this, you actually help everything lie flat. When you turn the piece and press the seam with your nail or iron it, it won't bunch up as badly.

Well, my goodness, that's an awful lot of blither blather to bore you with. I really hope you've skipped these pages and jumped ahead to Making Mouse (page 15). But if for some reason you have endured my nattering on, it is now really, really time to get started. We've got Mouse to make, and we've not a moment to lose!

Making Mouse

Before you have any adventures, you need to make Mouse! I will tell you that this pattern is the hardest one in the book. It has a lot of steps because Mouse has a lot of pieces. But don't worry—I'll be with you every step of the way. We'll do each step together so you won't get lost or frustrated. Ready?

GETTING STARTED

Start by picking your fabric. Do you want a soft and furry Mouse? A wild and colorful Mouse? I'm going to make a white Mouse with pink ears. The pink is flannel and the white is ribbed cotton. You don't need much—less than a fat quarter's worth of fabric.

Now that you have your fabric, go to pattern pullout page P1 and hunt up the seven pattern pieces you need to make Mouse. You're looking for Mouse's side body, chest, bottom, ear, foot, arm, and tail. We'll trace the three main body pieces first. Here are the patterns I made for Mouse's side body, bottom, and chest.

You should also find a pen so you can trace the patterns onto the back of your fabric. Test a few pens on a scrap of your fabric to make sure that the marker won't bleed through.

GETTING THE PIECES READY

1. Trace the pattern pieces onto the back of your fabric. Start by layering 2 small pieces of fabric and tracing the side body pattern. When you cut this out, you'll have the 2 side body pieces you need.

2. You'll only need 1 chest and 1 bottom, so trace and cut those out of a single layer of fabric.

THINGS YOU'LL NEED
- **White ribbed cotton:** scraps
- **Pink flannel (for inside ears):** small scrap
- **Polyfill**
- **Rice (*optional*)**
- **2 black seed beads**
- **Thick thread:** 8"–12" (20cm–30cm)

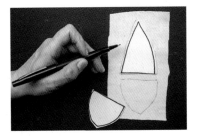

Here are the 4 main pieces: the 2 side bodies, the chest, and the bottom.

MAKING MOUSE'S EARS

1. Set aside the body parts for a moment, and let's focus on Mouse's ears. To make Mouse's ears you need a small rectangle of each type of fabric. Place them right sides together.

2. Trace around the ear pattern 2 times and sew on the line you drew. Remember to backstitch. Or you can free sew 2 little ears. This isn't hard; it's like sewing 2 U's. I've done it in pink thread so you can see how it's done. (You should use a matching thread, though, so your stitches won't show!)

3. Trim away the excess material and then turn the ears right side out. Try using the end of a pencil or a chopstick if you're having trouble getting them to turn. In this photo, the left ear has been turned, but the right ear hasn't yet. You'll see that there's a white side and a pink side.

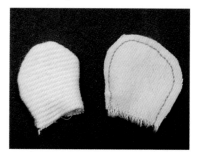

ATTACHING MOUSE'S EARS

1. Now you want to attach Mouse's ears to his head. His head is at the top of the side body pieces. I'm not going to lie... this next bit is tricky. You want to insert the ears into Mouse's head and sew them in place. One way to do this is to cut a little slit—about ½" (1.3cm) long—into both head pieces. There's a line on the pattern showing you where to put this ear slit. If you stack the body pieces, you can cut through both at the same place. Mark the spot where you want to cut using a ruler and pen.

2. Slowly and gently insert the tip of your scissors at the end of this line and snip along the line. This will create a tiny hole for you to slide the ear in place.

3. I usually bend a corner of the ear to get it to fit.

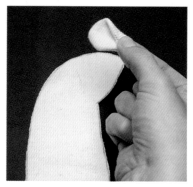

Here, I'm holding the ear in place so you can see what it will look like after you sew it.

4. Sew an ear in place. Here's what a single ear looks like from the wrong side.

5. Repeat! Ears for both sides!

SEWING TOGETHER MOUSE'S BODY

1. How are you holding up? I think you're doing really well so far. Now let's work on sewing Mouse's body together, okay? With right sides together, slowly stitch from the bottom of his chin all the way around his head and down his back, stitching about ¼" (0.6cm) from the edge. Make sure the ears are tucked away inside so you don't accidentally sew them down. I'm not going to tell you how many times I've done that!

If you want, go ahead and turn him right side out for a second. Awwwww… He's looking more Mouse-like every minute.

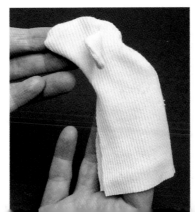

2. Let's keep going! Turn him inside out again. You've got to attach his chest. Do 1 side first and then the other. With right sides together, sew on the chest piece, starting from Mouse's neck and going down to the bottom of his body.

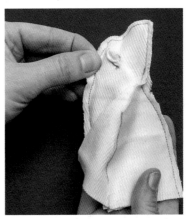

3. Good, good. Now the other side, too. Way to go!

In a minute, you're going to attach his bottom. But first, make this Mouse some feet.

ADDING THE FEET AND BOTTOM PIECE

1. This part is easy-peasy. Just cut out a small rectangle from the body fabric, fold it in half, and trace around the foot pattern 2 times. Stitch on the line you drew or free stitch 2 long U's.

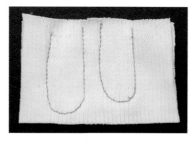

2. Trim the excess and gently turn—2 feet!

3. You should have another main body piece. It looks a little bit like a triangle with rounded sides. This goes on the bottom of Mouse.

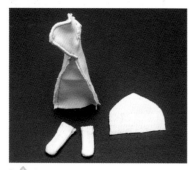

4. When you sew it in place, you're going to stitch the feet in place, too. Sandwich the feet between Mouse's front and the bottom piece. Point the feet in, so they face the center of the body. Place the bottom piece on top, with right sides together.

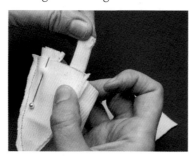

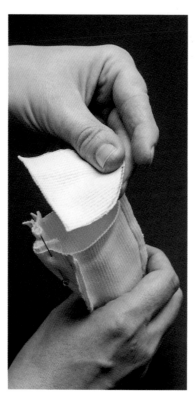

5. Stitch across the feet with a ¼" (0.6cm) seam.

If you peek, you can see the feet hidden inside.

6. Close it up again. No more peeking. Stitch the second side. Stitch some of the third side but leave a bit open to turn Mouse right side out.

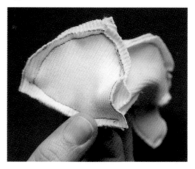

7. Stitch part of the third side, then backstitch. You're going to leave a small gap in this last side. Gently turn Mouse right side out.

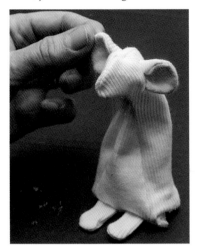

STUFFING MOUSE

1. Go ahead and stuff him with polyfill. This is where you could fill the bottom ½" (1.3cm) of him with rice. Only if you want to. Using just polyfill is perfectly fine, too.

2. Carefully stitch up the open gap by hand, using a matching thread.

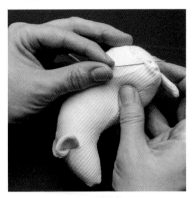

MAKING A TAIL FOR MOUSE

1. Mouse needs a tail, but that's easy enough! Cut a skinny rectangle and fold it in half. Trace around the tail pattern and stitch on the line you drew, or just sew a long, skinny U.

2. Trim the excess and turn.

3. Use a matching thread to stitch the tail to his *posterior*. That's a fancy way of saying his butt. You could also say fanny, rump, tush, or backend, but it's all the same, really.

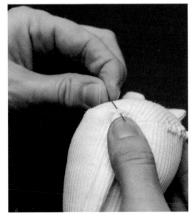

ADDING ARMS

1. You are doing an *awesome* job! Now you need to make 2 arms for your friend Mouse. Fold a large rectangle in half and trace around the arm pattern 2 times and stitch on the line you drew, or free sew 2 arms. I made mine like this:

2. Trim the excess and turn. Remember to use a pencil or chopstick if you're having trouble with turning.

3. We need to attach Mouse's arms to his body, 1 on each side, of course! Tuck under the raw edges and use a slip stitch to sew on each arm.

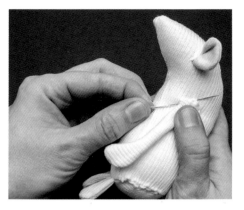

FINISHING UP

1. Let's give Mouse some eyes. I used tiny black seed beads.

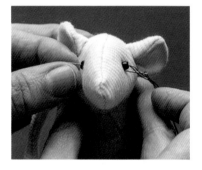

2. Only one thing missing ... whiskers! Use thick thread and feed it through his nose like this:

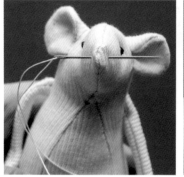 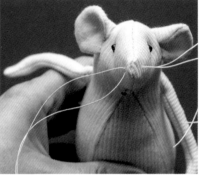

---

3. Then tie a knot on each end.

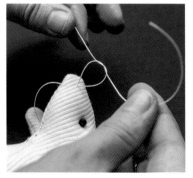

4. A quick trim and ...

... you did it! He looks great! Mouse is ready to begin his adventures.

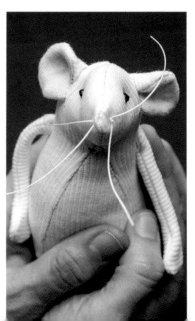

This Is Mouse—An Adventure in Sewing

On Safari

Let's go to Africa. But first Mouse needs some gear, including a leaf boat so he can sail downriver. Who will he meet along the way?

Jungle Gear

HAT

There's all sorts of weather to contend with in the jungle—from the scorching sun to drenching rains. Let's give Mouse a decent hat to protect him from the elements. You can make it out of brown felt. Check your pattern pullout page P1 for the three pattern pieces you'll need.

1. Trace the patterns and cut the pieces of brown felt on the line you traced. Make a tube out of the long, skinny piece. Overlap the ends just a bit and sew together by hand, using a matching thread.

2. Sew the top of the hat onto the tube, with about an ⅛″ (0.3cm) seam.

3. Now sew the hat top to the brim. And then turn it right side out.

That should shield Mouse from the sun and rain!

THINGS YOU'LL NEED
■ **Brown felt:** scraps

SATCHEL

THINGS YOU'LL NEED
- **Fake leather:** scrap
- **Thin cording:** at least 6" (15cm)

1. Cut a strip that's about 1½" (3.8cm) wide and 5" (13cm) long.

2. You need a length of cording or fake leather for the shoulder strap. Mine is vaguely labeled "fashion trim," but I chose it because it looks like fake leather and matches the fabric for the satchel.

All explorers and adventurers carry supplies with them. We'd best make a bag for Mouse to carry things in. It's not a *purse*, exactly. Let's call it a satchel and make it out of manly fake leather.

3. Turn over the fabric strip and fold up the bottom segment, right sides together, like so. Cut a length of cord for the strap, maybe 6" or 7" (15cm or 18cm), whatever works for your satchel.

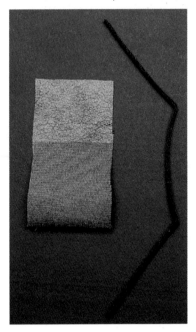

4. Before you sew the sides of the satchel and the strap in place, align everything and pin like this.

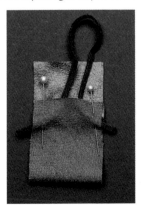

5. When you stitch it, give the satchel a rounded bottom. Note the backstitching at each end of the stitching.

6. Turn it right side out and trim the top edge of the satchel so that it curves.

7. Fold down the flap.

8. Mouse can throw it over his shoulder.

- -

MAP

It's easy to get lost, especially in a jungle. Let's send Mouse off on his adventure with a map.

You can draw your own map or cut up an old map. Make sure no one in your house needs the old map before you start cutting it up, though! I've got an old map of Costa Rica that I'm going to use.

1. Just cut a small section of the map. It only needs to be about 2" (5cm) tall and 5" (13cm) wide.

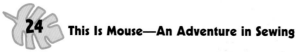

2. Now fold your map accordion-style. Mouse can use it as he travels.

LEAF BOAT

Mouse needs a sturdy vessel to go down the river. Why don't you make him a felt leaf boat? You need two sheets of felt, in any color you like; I've chosen two shades of green.

THINGS YOU'LL NEED

■ **Felt:** 2 pieces 9" × 12" (22.9cm × 30.5cm), green or whatever color you want

1. Stack the 2 sheets of felt on top of each other and trace the pattern from pattern pullout page P1.

2. Go ahead and cut your leaves out right on the line.

3. If you've ever looked closely at a leaf, you'll notice that it has veins running through it. Create those here by stitching a curving line down the center of the stacked pieces of felt. Add a few lines off the centerline, too.

4. Now take a little tour all around the outside of your leaf with a tight zigzag stitch. This stitch will seal the layers together and create a nice edge to the boat.

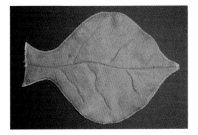

5. Grab your boat by both ends and pinch. Continue with the tight zigzag stitch along the edge at these 2 points.

The finished boat looks pretty good.

LEAN-TO

The jungle is a wild place, and if Mouse is going to spend any time there at all, he'll need a shelter. Let's build him a leaf lean-to. You need three squares of dark green felt and three squares of light green felt. Check pattern pullout page P1 for leaf patterns.

1. You'll need to cut and sew 8 skinny leaves and 1 fat leaf. To make these leaves, cut the felt sheets into strips. Let's get started with the first leaf. Each leaf will have a dark side and a light side.

2. Trace the skinny leaf template onto the top layer of felt.

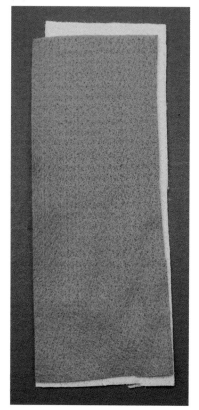

THINGS YOU'LL NEED

- **Felt:** 6 pieces 9" × 12" (22.9cm × 30.5cm), in 2 shades of green (3 of each)
- **Twine:** about 3 yards (3m)
- **Sticks:** 4 about 6" (15.2cm) long, and 4 about 10" (25.4cm) long

3. Cut out both pieces of your first leaf right on the line.

4. All leaves have veins. Sew a vein down the center of the layered pieces of felt and add a few off-shooting veins to the sides. I'm using a lime green thread so you can see it well.

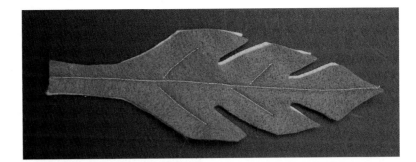

5. To make sure the 2 layers are sewn together firmly, outline the leaf using a tight zigzag stitch on the machine.

Terrific! Your first leaf is done. Each side of the lean-to needs 4 leaves. I've got 4 done now. How are you doing?

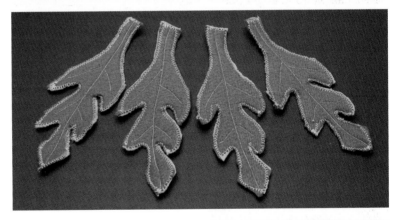

7. Wow! This takes *forever*! You need to have 8 skinny leaves in all, so keep sewing. We can talk while you work. Do you want to talk about your feelings? That's always good. Hmmm … you are feeling irritated with me because I'm making you sew so many leaves? Oh. Not good. Hey! Look at the time! You're done already—8 beautiful skinny leaves. Mouse will love this.

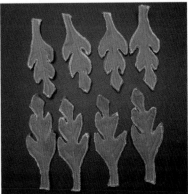

8. At the risk of having you hate me forever, you need to make *1 more leaf*—using the larger leaf pattern this time.

9. Follow the same drill for cutting it out…

10. … and sewing the veins and zigzagging the edges. Nicely done! You're a leaf pro now!

11. Now, the fun part. Ha! You are thinking, "There had *better* be a fun part to this." Find some twine (or yarn) and some sticks (or pencils or chopsticks or anything stick-like). You need 4 long sticks and 4 short ones— you can make your lean-to any size. My longest sticks are about 10" (25cm), and the shorter ones are about 6" (15cm).

12. Get ready to tie the tops of the leaves to a long stick.

13. Go ahead and tie 4 leaves to the first long stick.

14. Good, good. Now tie the bottoms of the leaves to the second long stick. This is the first side of Mouse's lean-to.

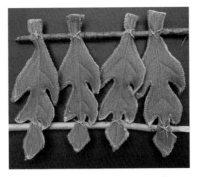

15. Take the other 4 skinny leaves and do the same with the other 2 long sticks. Now you have both sides of your lean-to.

16. Now take 2 of the short sticks and tie the sides of the lean-to at the 4 intersecting points. Don't worry if things feel a bit wobbly at this stage; you're about to shore everything up.

17. Flip over the lean-to and use the 2 remaining short sticks to connect the bottom of the lean-to at the intersecting points.

18. Add the fat leaf to the top of the lean-to. Put Mouse inside!

Crocodile

Finished size: about 21″ (53cm) long

Mouse is sure to see Crocodiles in the river, so we'll need to make some.

Look through your fabric stash and see if you can find a fabric suitable for Crocodile. If you're a traditionalist, you can stick with the green family. Look for something with a pattern, though. Using a plain color is a bit boring, and a pattern suggests texture. Croc's skin is on the bumpy side.

I'm going to try this wild purple.

1. It's up to you if you want to use my pattern (on pattern pullout page P1). There's only 1 pattern piece. You cut 2, a front and a back. If you want to try to create a Croc on your own, I say go for it. Crocs are long and skinny. They have 4 tiny legs and 2 bumps for eyes.

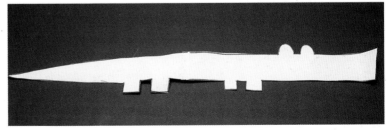

2. Fold your fabric in half and trace the pattern or just draw something remotely Croc-like on the back of your fabric.

3. PUT DOWN THOSE SCISSORS! Ye gods. Not yet, not yet. Here's a better idea: try sewing the pieces *first*. I've found that this makes life a little easier because you're not wrangling the skinny legs while sewing. Just follow your drawn line. Be sure to use a matching thread when you sew and not the lime green I've got going on here.

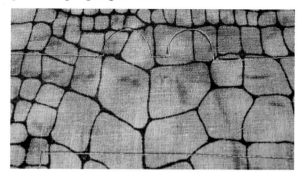

4. Remember to leave a wee bit of a gap as you sew so you can turn Croc right side out and stuff him. The gap can be anywhere, really, but I often leave it on his underbelly, between the 2 sets of legs. You might want to backstitch on either side of the gap. This adds strength for when you turn and stuff.

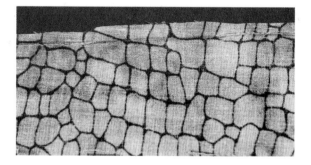

5. Now that you've sewn him, go ahead and cut him out, cutting about ¼" outside the stitching. See how easy that was?

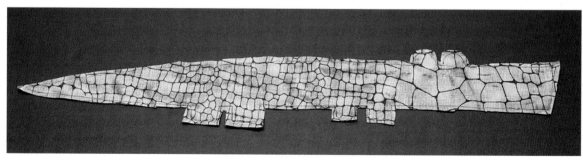

6. But, before you turn Croc, let's do a little snipping (see Clipping Curves, page 14). You see what I'm doing here? *Snip, snip, snippity snip.* I'm just making little cuts that follow along the curve of the eye. And why on earth am I doing that, you ask? Well, because it will make the whole job of turning easier. The eye will lie flat instead of bunching up. Just be sure you aren't cutting into your line of stitches, though, or else the whole thing will unravel hideously, and you'll be forced to repeat parts of Steps 1–5, muttering at me under your breath the whole while.

You also want to trim around Croc's legs, snipping off triangles at each corner, for the same reason.

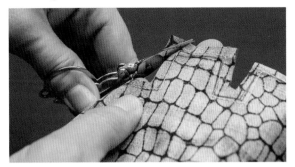

7. *Now* you can turn Croc. You may need to use a pencil or other jabby tool to push out his tail and legs. Go gently, though, especially on the legs. If you push too hard, you'll blow the stitches.

8. Ah, yes, he's looking pretty good here, I'd say.

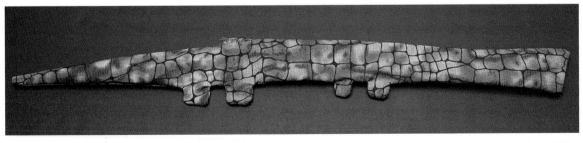

9. Now for the *dangerous* part: stuffing him. What's life without a little danger, eh? Assuming you didn't blow out any legs on the turning, you run the risk of doing so now. I'm not going to tell you how many legs I've blown out on how many Crocodiles or how many oaths have been muttered as a result. So, it does happen. But if *you* are careful, you can get through this. Start with the tail and work your way forward. When you get to the legs, go slowly. Don't force anything. Watch those eyeballs, too. Gentle, gentle, gentle.

10. Make sure Croc is firmly stuffed. If you hold him upright, he should be stiff as a board and not flop. When Croc is stuffed, use a matching thread to sew up the little gap.

11. Eyes! I'm going to use 2 tiny black seed beads. You can try beads, sequins, felt—whatever feels right.

12. Hand stitch the eyes in place.

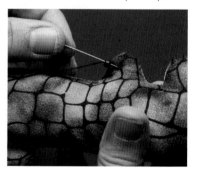

He's all done, ready to menace the jungle!

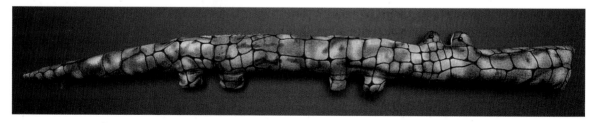

You can make your Croc look very different by
adding a little rickrack. I've used it as teeth   or as spines on his back.

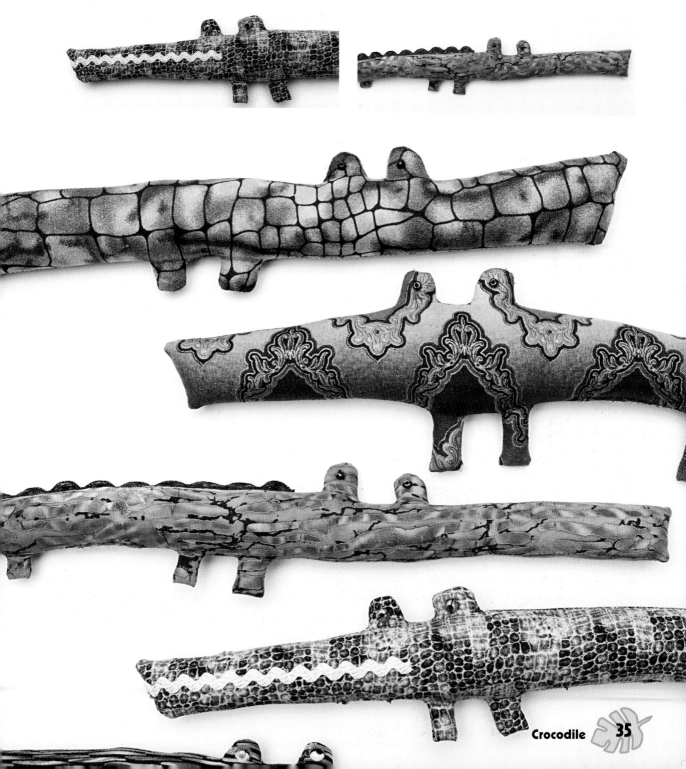

Elephant

I think elephants, in the wild anyway, might be gray. Gray is a little boring, so you'll not see any gray Elephants in this book. If *you* need a gray Elephant, then by all means make one. But otherwise, you might try something a little more colorful, such as one of these fabrics.

THINGS YOU'LL NEED

- **Fabric:** ¼ yard or fat quarter
- **Polyfill**
- **Yarn, ribbon, rope, or tassel:** about 2" (5cm) long
- **2 buttons**

I've settled on this disturbingly bright orange cotton. Rather lively, I think. This Elephant won't be hard to spot in the jungle.

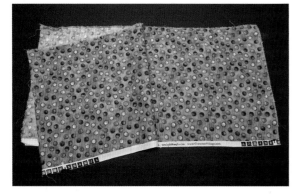

1. You'll need to consult Ye Ol' Patterns (pullout page P1) for the Elephant bits. You'll be happy to know that unlike Mouse, which has eleventy-billion small pieces, Elephant has only 3 pattern pieces. You could also shrink the patterns on a photocopy machine to make baby elephants.

2. Go ahead and trace the pattern pieces onto the back of your fabric. Remember, you need 2 body pieces, 4 ear pieces, and 1 underbelly piece.

3. When you've gotten everything marked, cut out your pieces on the line.

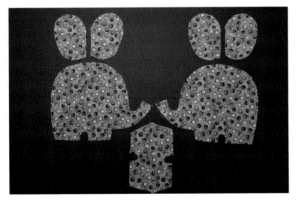

4. Start sewing with the ears. With right sides together, stitch all the way around the curved part of each pair with a ¼" (0.6cm) seam. Leave open the flat side so you can turn the ears.

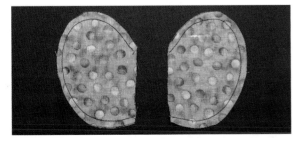

5. Before you turn the ears, though, do the snipping thing and clip the curves (see Clipping Curves, page 14). *Snip, snip, snippity snip.* Just make cuts that follow along the curve of the ear. I'm doing this so the ear will lie flat instead of bunching up when I turn it.

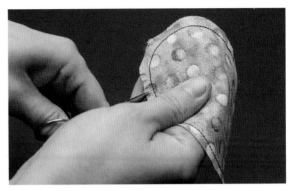

6. Give the ears a turn now. Use your nail to crease the edges if there are any lumpy parts.

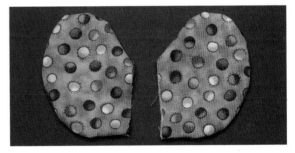

7. You want to insert each ear into Elephant's head.

8. Start by marking a line on Elephant's head with a ruler and pen where you want to cut.

9. To cut, gently insert the tip of your scissors at the end of the line.

10. Cut along the line.

11. Now slide an ear into place.

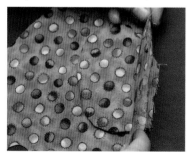

12. Next, stitch a line straight across the opening to secure the ear in place.

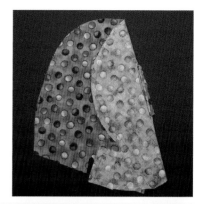

13. Remember to do this ninja move for both body pieces. It should look something like this.

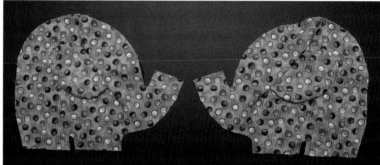

14. Excellent! Now to sew the body pieces together. With right sides together, and still with that ¼" (0.6cm) seam, stitch from the bottom of the trunk—where my right hand is—all the way around Elephant's back and down his backside, but not his leg. Stop where you see my left hand is. BUT! Before you do this, there's another important thing to tell you.

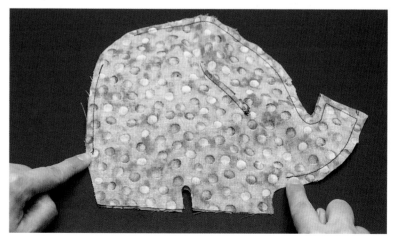

15. You also need to leave a little gap at the top of Elephant's back. See where my fingers are? Backstitch on either side of this gap—this is where you stuff him after you've sewn on his underbelly. But …

16. … don't go any further until you do that *snippity-snip-snip* thing again around the curves, okay?

17. *Now* to sew on his underbelly. Make sure you line up this piece so that the right side of the fabric is facing in.

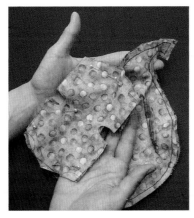

18. Go ahead and stitch all the way around that sucker, still with a ¼″ (0.6cm) seam. No worries, remember, because you left a gap on the top for turning and stuffing.

19. *Snip, snip, snippity snip* those curves. I know I sound like a broken record about that, but it will really make a difference when you turn him.

20. So let's do that now! Turn him! Wheeeeeeee!

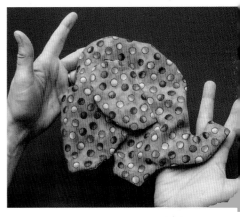

21. You'll need some polyfill to stuff him. Start with his trunk first. Pack tightly. Stuff the head and front legs. The legs will drive you crazy because they aren't very big, so the polyfill will want to keep popping out. You must use a firm hand here and show that polyfill who is boss. Try using polite but firm language. Something along the lines of: "Take *that*, pachyderm!"

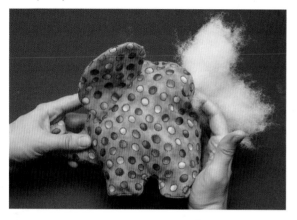

22. After you have Elephant firmly stuffed, stitch up the open gap. Use a matching thread to hide your stitches.

23. Elephant needs a tail. You can try all sorts of things—yarn, ribbon, rope. I'm going to use a little leather tassel that is about 2″ (5.1cm) long. Make yours whatever length you want.

24. Gently stitch the tail in place.

25. He needs eyes as well. I've got a couple of small, sparkly buttons. What do you have?

26. Hand stitch on the eyes with matching thread.

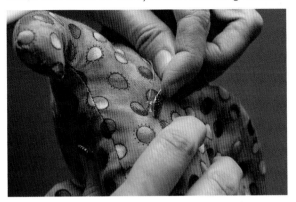

And Bob's your uncle! What a fine-looking Elephant!

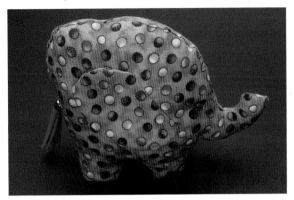

You can have a lot of variety with Elephants depending on what fabrics you choose and what kinds of tails you put on and how big you make them. You can shrink or enlarge the pattern on a copier to change the size of the Elephant.

Giraffe

No jungle would be complete without a few giraffes. You might be thinking that giraffes are generally brown. And generally, they are. But in Mouse's world, Giraffes can be anything, including blue.

THINGS YOU'LL NEED

- **Fabric:** ¼ yard or fat quarter
- **Polyfill**
- **2 small beads**

I don't really know what you call those shapes on Giraffe's skin—blobs? Blotches? Swatches? Specks? Well, whatever they are, I've found an interesting purple corduroy with turquoise whatchacallits on it. It looks Giraffe-y to me.

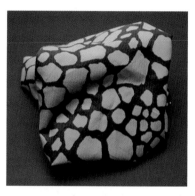

1. Whip out your pattern pullout page P1 and let's have a go at this. You need 2 side bodies and 2 underbodies.

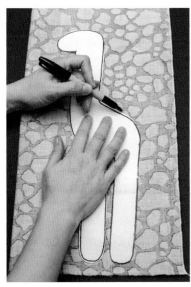

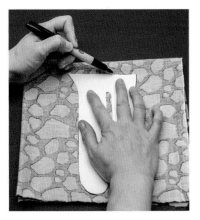

2. After tracing the patterns, cut them out on the line.

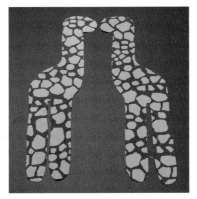

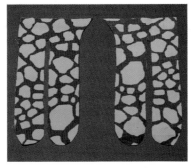

3. Well, it's nice to have the main bits and pieces, but what about Giraffe's ears, you ask? Fair enough. She'll need 2 ears, but I think you can free sew them. It's not hard. Just snip off a little rectangle of fabric, oh, probably 2" long and 1½" high or so (5.1cm × 1.3cm).

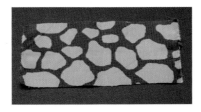

4. Fold this bit in half and free sew 2 long, pointy Giraffe ears, or trace the pattern, stitching on the line.

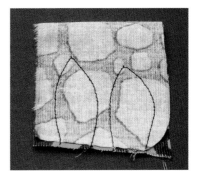

5. Trim and turn said ears.

6. That's lovely. Now you need to get ready to attach the ears. Use a pen and ruler to mark the spots where you want to cut.

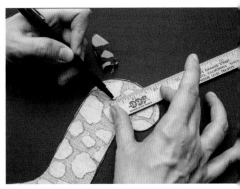

7. Gently insert the tip of your scissors at the end of the line you just drew and cut along the line.

8. You're going to slide in the ear, folding the top down just a bit,

and then stitch it in place.

9. Do this for each side.

10. Let's focus on Giraffe's underbelly for a second now. With right sides together, stitch together the 2 pieces across the top with a ¼" (0.6cm) seam.

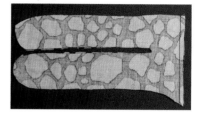

11. If you open up this piece, you get what looks like a colorful moth. Or maybe you see something else. We could use this as a Rorschach test—you can tell me what you see and how it makes you feel. How long have you had an unresolved fear of brussels sprouts? Perfectly understandable, if you ask me. *Nasty* things, they are. But wait! We digress! There's no time for this nonsense. We must keep moving.

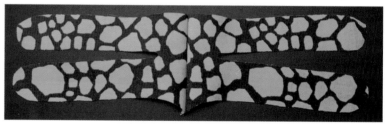

12. Set aside the underbody for a moment and go back to the side body pieces. With right sides together and starting at the base of the neck, begin sewing together the pieces, again with a ¼" (0.6cm) seam. Sew all the way around the head and down Giraffe's back, and stop at the dot at the tail.

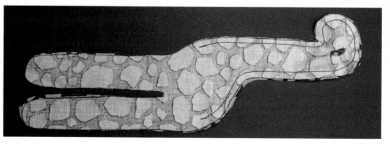

13. Now get ready to put everything together. I used 7 gazillion pins to line up the underbody with the sides (well, maybe not quite that many). You can probably use fewer pins, but *why take the risk*, I ask you?

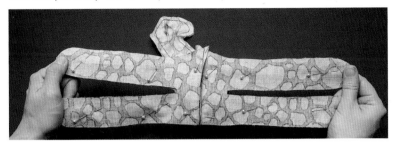

14. Slowly stitch all the way around the underbody, but leave a small opening at Giraffe's butt so that you can turn her. Remember to backstitch at this opening.

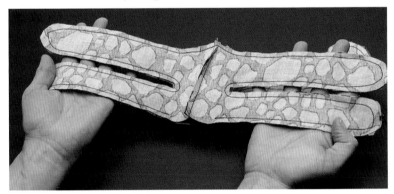

15. Turn Giraffe and smooth out any wrinkles. If you run into any bad lumps, you might need to turn her inside out again and do some *snip, snip, snipping* on the curves.

16. Begin stuffing the ol' girl. Now, I'm not going to lie; stuffing Giraffe legs is not for the faint of heart—no sir. It's slow and frustrating work. You have to pack the polyfill tightly, but if you push too hard, you'll blow a seam. So I want you to get started on this, but in a few minutes, take a break. I'm not kidding. In a few minutes, take a break. Look at pictures of baby animals until your blood pressure goes down; then go back to packing those legs. If done right, the process will only take 6 hours or so, but Giraffe will have great legs AND you'll have your sanity!

17. When you're all set, stitch the small gap that you left open to turn and stuff her with.

18. Ah, looking good now!

19. A pair of eyes are needed to finish her off. I've got a couple of small beads here I'm going to try.

20. Stitch on the eyes with a matching thread.

Beautiful!

To make a baby giraffe, shrink the pattern on a photocopy machine. But watch those legs—they can get really skinny!

Snake

There be Snakes in the jungle. Lots and lots of them. Let's make one now (you can make more later). It's fun to use super-shiny fabric for Snakes—silk, lamé, or foil knits.

THINGS YOU'LL NEED

- **Silk, lamé, or foil knit:** Snake-length scraps
- **Ribbon or cording** (*optional*)
- **Rice**
- **2 seed beads**

I'm going to use hot pink for a lady Snake.

Hissssssssssss.

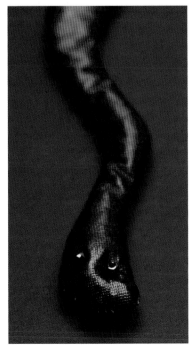

You can use the pattern on pullout page P1 or sew without—entirely up to you. There's only one pattern piece—you cut two, a front and a back. You can also just draw Snake on your own. She can be very curvy or straight as a line. She can be short or long, fat or skinny.

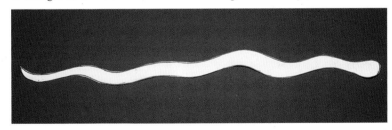

1. I'm going to trace my pattern on the back of the fabric. You trace or draw.

2. Don't worry about cutting out Snake yet. You'll have an easier time sewing both pieces of her if you just follow the lines you've drawn and cut her out after sewing.

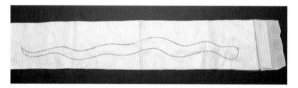

But before you sew, what if you want to add a tongue, you ask. Well, I've got that covered. Check out Making a Snake Tongue (page 50) before you go any further.

3. With Snake's front and back pieces right sides together, sew around the edges. Remember to leave a small gap so you can turn her and stuff her. You can leave the gap anywhere. Backstitching on either side of the gap to reinforce the edges of the opening is a good idea here.

4. Now you're ready to cut her out.

5. Take care of those curves before you turn her, eh? Just make small cuts around the curves. *Snip, snip, snippity snip.*

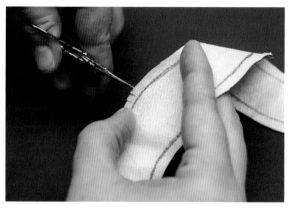

6. Okay, turn her now. If you are working with an odd fabric, you may be in for a slow time of it. My fabric is a bit sticky, so it's hard to turn her.

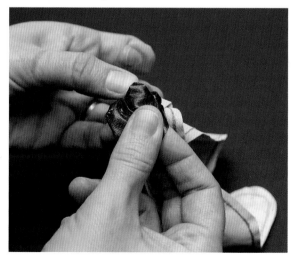

7. I'm going to use a pencil to gently jab the fabric through.

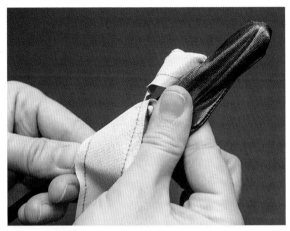

8. With enough BRUTE FORCE, er, I mean, gentle persuasion, she should finally turn.

9. You want Snake to be flexible, so don't stuff her with polyfill. Instead, try rice! I've got a little funnel that I like to use when doing this.

10. After you've loaded Snake up with rice, you're ready to close her.

11. With a matching thread, hand stitch the gap closed.

12. She's looking terrific!

13. Now to add some eyes. Tiny black seed beads will show up well against her pink skin.

14. Hand stitch the eyes in place.

You don't have to make just one Snake; you can make many more!

Making a Snake Tongue

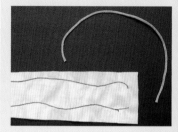

If you want to give your Snake a tongue to hiss with, it's easy enough to do.

1. Find a bit of ribbon or cording.

2. Insert the cording while you're sewing Snake's head, a few inches or longer. It's up to you.

3. When the tongue is inserted, just sew across Snake's head like you normally would.

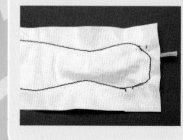

4. When you turn her, she'll look like this:

Now go back to Snake, Step 3 (page 48) and pick up where you left off.

🍃 Mouse Goes on Safari 🍃

Now that you've got all the pieces made, it's time for an adventure!

Mouse is ready to go. He has his map, his satchel, his hat, and his very fine leaf boat. He sets off downriver, but he hasn't traveled long before he feels like he is being watched.

He had heard these were Crocodile-infested waters, but he wasn't prepared for this! Maybe it's time to abandon ship before these "friendly" Crocs capsize the boat.

Mouse makes his way into the jungle and builds his leaf lean-to. Before long, he hears a rustling outside.

Good grief! It's a full-size Elephant. Do Elephants eat mice? This one seems to like Mouse's hat.

It turns out that Elephant couldn't be nicer. He introduces Mouse to the other Elephants. They entertain Mouse with interesting stories and amazing feats.

After a time, Mouse leaves the Elephants and wanders deeper into the jungle. Here the tree trunks are all sorts of funny colors.

Wait a second! Those aren't tree trunks. Mouse is standing in a forest of Giraffes!

A tall Giraffe offers to give Mouse a ride so that he can see the whole jungle.

It's an amazing sight. In the distance, Mouse can see many jungle vines. He wonders what it would be like to swing on them like a monkey.

The vines are very colorful. Mouse loves swinging on them.

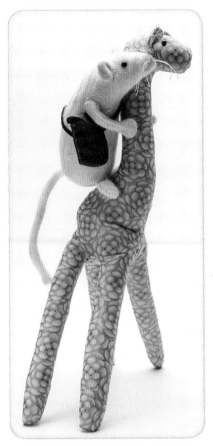

Hold on a minute! Why does this vine have EYES?

Great snakes! These vines are Snakes!

Mouse knows that Snakes like Mice. Maybe a little too much. It's time to leave the jungle and begin a new adventure!

Deep Freeze

The South Pole is a cold and desolate place. A little white mouse like Mouse might get lost in a frozen place like this. Mouse needs to be prepared!

Cold Weather Gear

SCARF

To keep Mouse warm in the South Pole, you'll need to make him a few things, such as a scarf.

1. This is easy to make. Cut a small strip of flannel or fleece. I've made mine about 9" (18cm) long and 1" (2.5cm) wide.

2. Fringe the ends by making small, thin cuts.

And now it's ready to wear!

THINGS YOU'LL NEED
- **Flannel or fleece:** scraps

EARMUFFS

Mouse will appreciate the scarf, but I think he'll also like earmuffs.

1. Dig through your stash and see if you can find some very thin ribbon—¼" (0.6cm) wide. Also look for 2 tiny pom-poms.

THINGS YOU'LL NEED
- **Ribbon:** a few inches
- **2 mini pom-poms**
- **Hot glue gun**

2. Cut a length of ribbon 1½" (3.8cm) long. Use a hot glue gun (mind your fingers!) to attach the pom-poms to the ends of the ribbon.

3. Drape the earmuffs across Mouse's head.

THINGS YOU'LL NEED

- **7 foam or wood craft sticks:** each about 6″ × ¾″ (15.2cm × 1.9cm)
- **Hot glue gun**
- **Twine or yarn:** about 5′ (1.5m)

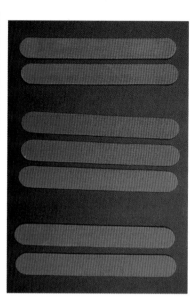

SLED

Getting around in all that snow and ice will be no easy task. Mouse needs a decent sled. You can make one for him out of craft sticks or tongue depressors. Wooden sticks work fine for this, but I'm going to use the foam ones because they are easier to cut. You need seven sticks—each about 6″ × ¾″ (15.2cm × 1.9cm). Red ones will be good— easier for Mouse to spot in the snow.

1. Start with 3 sticks. Cut off the rounded tips of each.

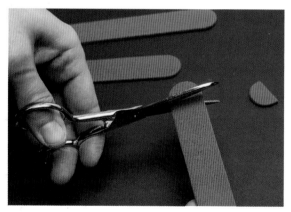

2. Now cut those pieces in half. You should have 6 pieces of equal length. These will be the baseboard for the sled.

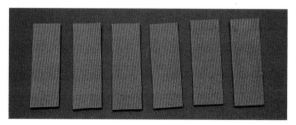

3. Good. Now take 2 sticks from your remaining pile.

4. Using the sled rail pattern from your pattern pullout page P2, trim 2 more sticks. These are the upright pieces that will help stabilize the sled. Don't throw away the middle sections that you cut out, though. You'll use them, too—2 will be supports and the long piece will be the crossbar.

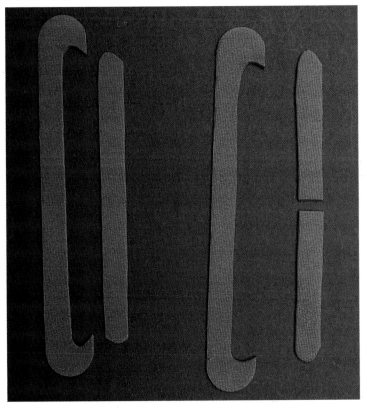

5. Cut your last 2 sticks following the sled runner pattern. Trim them to make them look like the runners, or bottom pieces, of the sled. These are the pieces that slide on the ice.

6. Now to assemble the sled. Whip out your hot glue gun (mind your fingers). You only need 5 sections to make up the baseboard. Line them up. Put a bead of glue on the edges of the runners and stick them to the baseboard pieces.

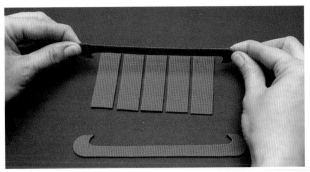

7. After the glue dries, you can flip the piece over to see the beginnings of your sled.

8. Go ahead and glue the uprights and their 2 supports next.

9. Add the final piece to the sled—the crossbar.

10. Mouse is ready, but he can't go anywhere yet. You have to set up the rigging to the sled and find some Able-Bodied Volunteers to pull it.

11. Go ahead and set the sled up for 3 Able-Bodied Volunteers, but you can attach as many leads as you like. Cut 1 long piece of twine, maybe 20" (51cm) long. That will be your main rope. Tie a slipknot at each end. Then cut 3 slightly shorter lengths of twine—around 12" (31cm) each. These are your lead lines. Tie a large slipknot at an end of the lead lines. I hope you are remembering all this because there will be a quiz afterward, and you never know when you'll have to rig up a sled.

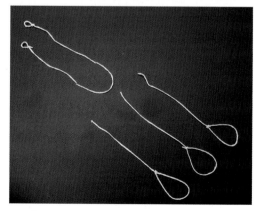

This Is Mouse—An Adventure in Sewing

How Do I Make a Slipknot?

1. It's not too hard. Make a little loop with your rope.

2. Bring the top piece of rope under the loop.

3. Pull this new loop through the first loop to tighten the knot.

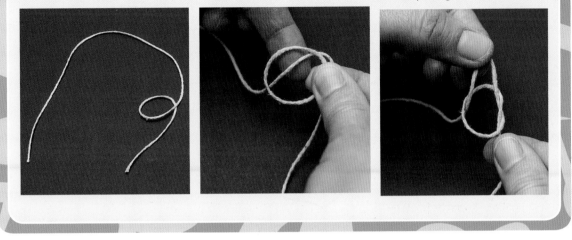

12. Cinch the slipknots from the lead rope to the ends of the sled's crossbar.

13. Now knot the leads to the main rope.

14. Harness up your volunteers by slipping the slipknots of the lead lines around their tummies! Hmmm … those don't look like sled dogs to me …

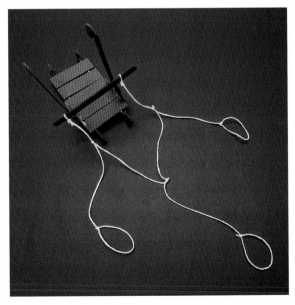

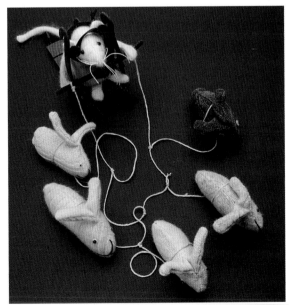

IGLOO

Good grief! It's cold in the South Pole. Even with his winter fur, earmuffs, and a scarf, Mouse is freezing his bits and pieces off. Good thing the Penguins are master builders of igloos. They'll show Mouse (and you!) what to do. You need some sugar cubes. A lot of sugar cubes, actually. I had two boxes on hand. Half a box went into a cup of tea, but the rest was needed for the igloo.

THINGS YOU'LL NEED
- **Sugar cubes:** 2 boxes
- **Hot glue gun**

1. First, trace my pattern (on pullout page P2) or make a little sketch for yourself. An igloo is roundish, with a short opening.

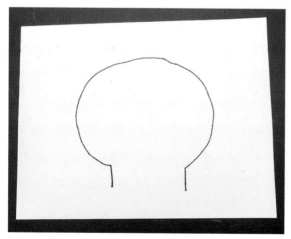

2. Now start placing sugar cubes on the outline you drew. Start with the bottom row and go all the way around. Crank up your hot glue gun while you're doing this step because you're going to need it soon. When you get the first row lined up on your sketch, you're ready to start stacking and gluing.

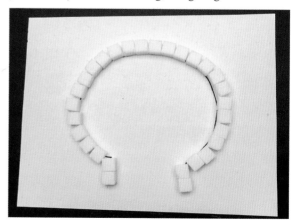

3. Glue each sugar cube down as you go. Mind those fingers! Do not *singe, singe, singe* your fingers. Here's what it looks like after a few rows.

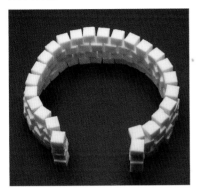

4. You'll notice that I'm not stacking the cubes perfectly on top of each other. There's space between the cubes, and some are turned at a slight angle. Place the cubes so that you keep the arc of the igloo going, and you're still able to glue the cubes together.

5. After 5 rows, start making the doorway. Notice how I staggered the front cubes inward a little until I was able to create a bridge across. I used a good deal of glue to make it all stick. I also scorched my fingers quite a bit, so do be careful.

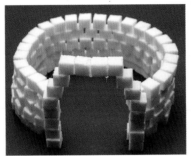

6. When you've got that bridge across, you can continue to build up, getting narrower as you go by setting in the cubes slightly each time.

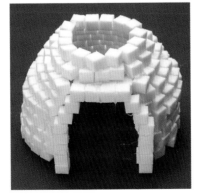

7. My igloo looks a bit like an ice pyramid here. You may not want to put a pointed top on your igloo; it's entirely up to you.

Mouse is very proud of the finished igloo!

Fish

Finished size: about 3″ (8cm) long

Oh, those Penguins! If they aren't building igloos, they are thinking about Fish. There are lots of ways you can make Fish. I'll show you one easy way.

THINGS YOU'LL NEED
- **Shiny fabric scraps**
- **Polyfill**

1. Find a little hunk of shiny fabric. I used the same sort of fabric I use to make a lot my Snakes. Careful, though—this fabric is slippery and can make for slippery Fish.

2. Cut a small square of your fabric and place it facedown. Put a pinch of polyfill on top.

3. Now fold over your fabric to make a sandwich. (A Fish sandwich—yum!)

4. Free sew the shape of Fish. I outlined my Fish using aqua thread and a zigzag stitch. It creates a thick line around Fish. There is a pattern (on pullout page P2) to trace if you prefer. Stitch right on the line.

5. Without cutting into any of your stitches, trim around Fish to get rid of the excess fabric.

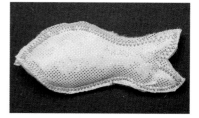

Rabbit

Finished size: about 2½" (6.4cm) tall (not including ears)

Whoever heard of a sled rabbit? Well, I don't know. Obviously these bunnies are a long way from home. But they don't seem to mind the weather or the work. Lucky for us, these bunnies are easy to make.

THINGS YOU'LL NEED

- **Fuzzy sock or fabric scraps**
- **Polyfill or rice**
- **2 wiggle eyes**
- **Embroidery floss:** 8"–10" (20cm–25cm)

You can make Rabbits out of any kind of fabric, but I made mine out of a fuzzy sock.

1. Find a fuzzy sock.

2. Cut off the cuff of the sock.

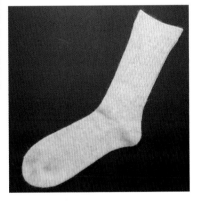

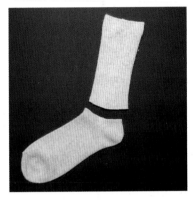

3. Next cut open the cuff.

4. Place it flat, like so.

5. Now fold it the other way.

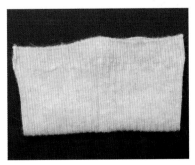

6. Place the Rabbit pattern (on pullout page P1) on top and trace around it.

7. Use another part of your sock to trace the ear pattern.

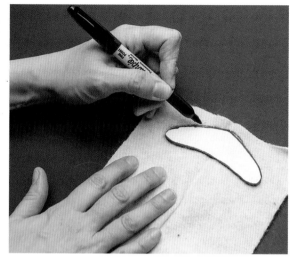

8. Now you're going to gently, gently, slowly, slowly stitch the outline of Rabbit, right on the line. But here's the weird thing—you're not going to stitch the ears yet. Also, note that I'm using a contrasting thread. *Don't* follow my lead on this—*you* want to use a matching thread. This guy is so small that if I didn't use a colorful thread, you'd never be able to see what I was doing!

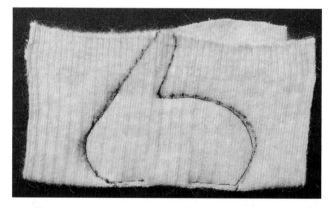

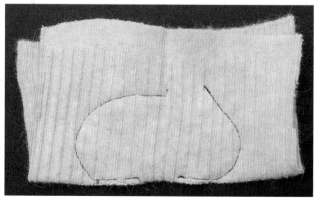

9. Trim away the excess sock.

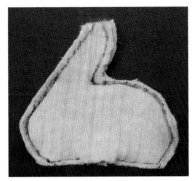

10. Cut out the ear that you traced earlier.

11. Get ready to sew the ear onto the body. Separate the unsewn ears on the rabbit and match them to the cut-out ear.

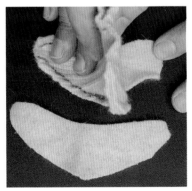

12. You might want to pin it in place, right sides together.

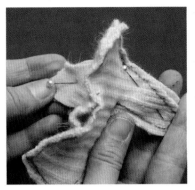

13. Stitch slowly and gently around the ears with a ¼" (0.6cm) seam.

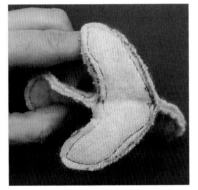

14. Turn Rabbit.

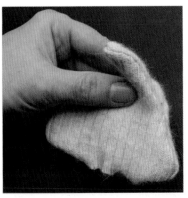

15. Stuff Rabbit. You can use a small amount of polyfill or try using rice. I used polyfill here. Using a matching thread, sew up the gap that you left for turning.

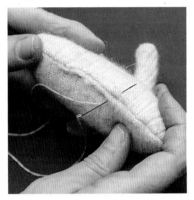

16. Looking good!

17. If you find that Rabbit's ears are sticking up and looking awkward, you can tack them down with just a few stitches. I usually do this in the front and in the back.

18. That's better!

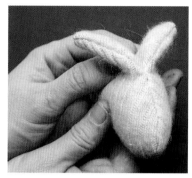

19. Your Rabbit needs a tail. You can use a tiny piece of leftover sock.

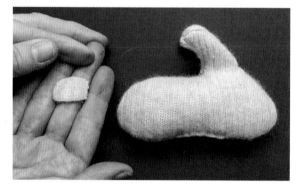

20. Make a small button out of it by folding the edges toward the center. Hold it against your Rabbit's rump and stitch it in place using a matching thread. Nicely done!

21. Your Rabbit can have any sort of eyes you like. I used the dreaded hot glue gun to put on these wiggle eyes. And, yes, I did scorch my fingers. Again. So do be careful with that thing if you use it.

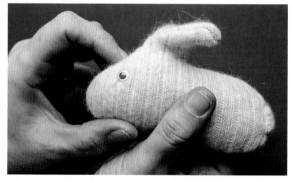

22. Use some embroidery floss to put a little nose and mouth on Rabbit.

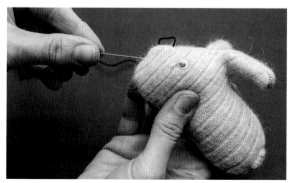

23. After you have a line for the nose, stitch across for half the mouth.

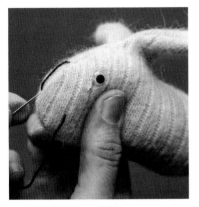

24. And across again for the other half.

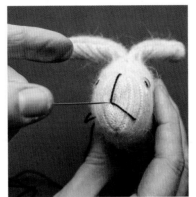

Perfect!

Make as many Rabbits as you need.

Penguin

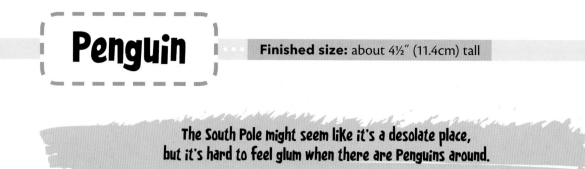

Finished size: about 4½″ (11.4cm) tall

The South Pole might seem like it's a desolate place,
but it's hard to feel glum when there are Penguins around.

We'll enter the world of black and white to make our Penguin.

THINGS YOU'LL NEED
- **Fabric scraps (black, white, and yellow)**
- **White gel pen**
- **Polyfill**
- **2 seed beads**

I like using a patterned black-and-white fabric for Penguin's tummy and a black fabric for his back. We'll also need a hint of yellow, for Mr. Penguin's beak.

Because you'll be working with a lot of dark fabric, try to use a white gel pen to mark the pattern.

1. Find Penguin's 4 different pattern pieces (on pullout page P2). You'll need 2 flippers in black, 2 flippers in patterned fabric, 2 black backs, 2 patterned tummies, and 1 black bottom.

2. Begin by tracing Penguin's back on the black fabric. Use a double layer of black because you need 2 black pieces. I'm using my white gel pen so I can see what I'm doing.

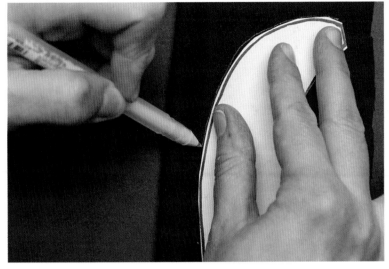

3. I'm going cut this out now, eyeballing about ¼" (0.6cm) outside my line. You can see what it looks like.

4. Next take the patterned fabric, use a double layer, and trace the tummy on it.

5. Cut out these tummy pieces, again, about ¼" (0.6cm) outside the line; you should have 2.

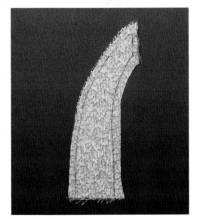

6. For each side of Penguin, you'll have a black back and a patterned tummy.

7. Now for the tricky bit: you need to attach the back and tummy. Place the tummy piece on top of the black piece. right sides together.

8. I know what you are thinking. You are thinking: "Great googly moogly! What ARE you telling me to do? This is all backward, and it doesn't fit." I hear you, my friend, and I know this is an unnatural move. But trust me—it's going to work out. Refer to Curve Madness (page 12) and sew gently and slowly from bottom to top, right on the line, pulling the fabric as you stitch until it lines up. It's going to look a bit like so:

9. When you open this up, crease along the seam to get it to lie flat. Now it looks perfect. See? Didn't I tell you?

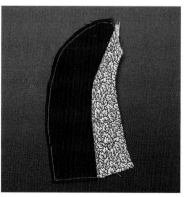

10. Do this move twice so that you have both sides of Penguin.

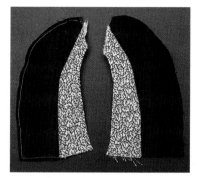

11. Penguin's beak comes next. Search your stash for a tiny bit of yellow or orange. You only need 2 small 1″ × 1″ (2.5cm × 2.5cm) squares.

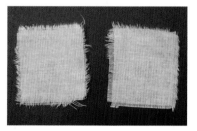

12. Place the first yellow square down across Penguin's face, right sides together, and sew it down, straight across.

13. When you fold it back, it should look like this. Follow this beak procedure for both sides.

14. Stack Penguin's body pieces right sides together and stitch, starting at the base of the tummy and sewing all the way around to Penguin's back. When you get to the yellow squares, sew a triangle to form the beak.

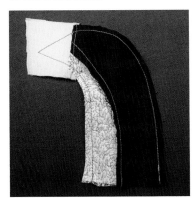

15. Gently trim away the excess fabric.

16. Put Penguin's body aside for a moment and use a white gel pen to trace around the round bottom piece.

17. Cut out Penguin's bottom, a bit outside of the line.

18. You're going to attach the bottom to Penguin. It's a bit like putting a round peg in a square hole, though.

19. I tend to do this maneuver by hand, although you can try to stitch the bottom in place using your machine. It's such a tiny piece that I feel I have better control when I do it by hand. Sew the bottom circle onto Penguin, leaving about a 1″ (2.5cm) gap for turning and stuffing.

20. After the bottom is in place, turn Penguin.

21. Now to stuff the little guy. Pack him tightly, but be careful of his beak. If you pack it too roughly, you can split the seam. (Ouch!) You could also add rice at the bottom ½″ (1.3cm) of him, if you want.

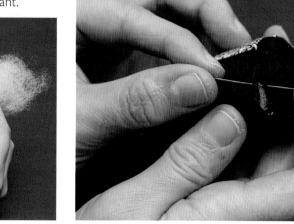

22. With matching thread, stitch by hand the small gap you left for turning.

23. You're getting there, but you do need to make a set of flippers for Penguin. He won't need them for flying, but he does need them to swim. Trace 2 complete sets of flippers from a layer of black and a layer of the patterned fabric.

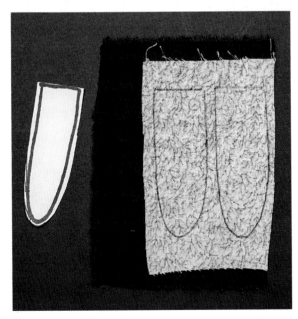

24. With right sides together, slowly stitch together the 2 layers. Be sure to leave the straight edges of the flippers open.

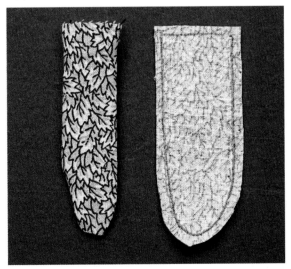

25. Trim away the excess fabric and turn each flipper.

26. Before you attach the flippers, Pengy needs some eyes. I'm using tiny black seed beads.

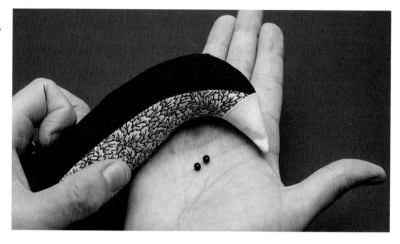

27. Sew the eyes onto the upper part of his yellow beak.

He's looking good!

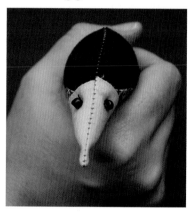

28. Now stitch the flippers onto the body, first 1 side, then the other. Be sure to tuck under the raw edges first, and use a slipstitch and a matching thread to hide your stitches.

He's ready for a swim in the frigid waters!

This Is Mouse—An Adventure in Sewing

Seal

Seals are often gray; their babies white. They can also be yellow, blue, or pink. Not really. But in our world, we will say that they can. Try something soft here, like flannel or a thin fur. The pieces are small, so you don't want to have to wrangle anything too thick.

THINGS YOU'LL NEED

- **Flannel or thin fur scraps**
- **Polyfill**
- **Thick thread:** about 8" (20.3cm)
- **2 seed beads**

I'm going with a white flannel, accented with pale blue dots. Not quite what you'd see in nature, but …

1. To make Seal, you only need 2 pattern pieces (on pullout page P2).

2. Trace the pattern pieces onto the back of your fabric. You need 2 body pieces and 1 underbelly.

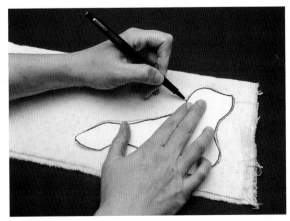

3. When you cut out your pieces right on the line, here's what you should have.

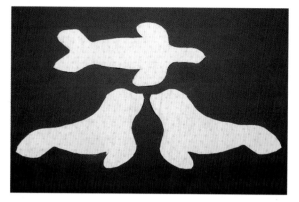

4. Put the side pieces right sides together. Stitch along the nose and the back of Seal's head with a ¼" (0.6cm) seam. Sew all the way down to the beginning point of her flippers.

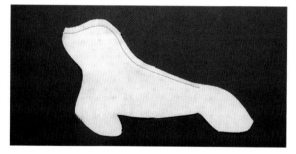

5. To attach the underbelly, stitch along a side. Start with the nose and sew all the way down Seal's body, around the front flipper, and around the back flipper.

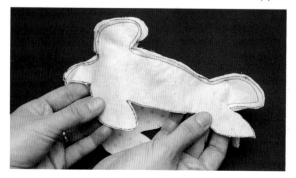

6. Do the same with the other side, leaving a 1" (2.5cm) gap in Seal's side so you can turn her.

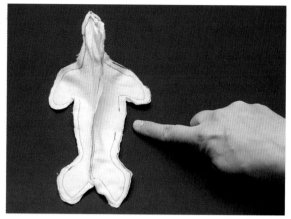

7. Carefully trim around the curved parts of her flippers. *Snip, snip, snippity snip.*

8. Turn Seal.

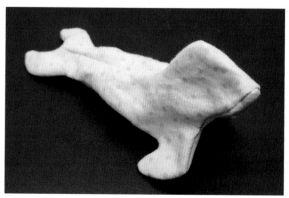

9. Begin stuffing her. Start with her back flippers and work your way forward to her head. Pack the stuffing fairly tightly, especially around the flippers.

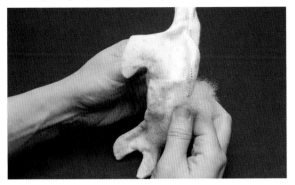

10. Once you've got her stuffed, stitch up the gap with a matching thread.

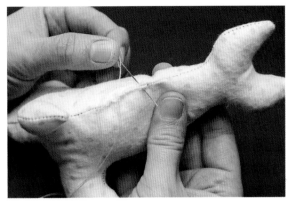

11. Now you've got eyes to consider. I usually go with small seed beads.

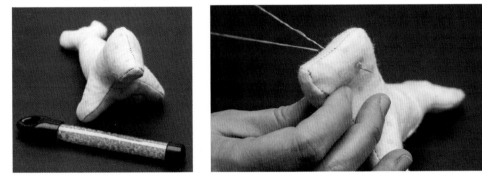

12. The only things missing now are a few whiskers. Use a thick thread and feed it through her nose.

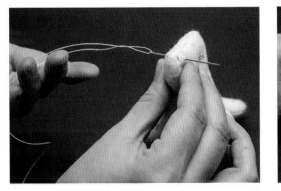

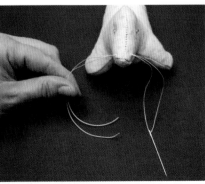

13. Knot the ends on both sides.

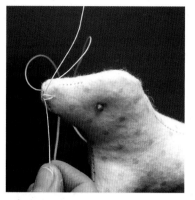

14. Give the whiskers a bit of a trim.

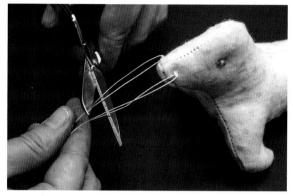

She's ready to hit the ice!

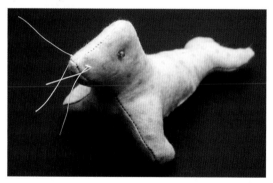

By shrinking the pattern down on a photocopy machine, you can make baby Seals.

Whale

Won't tiny Mouse be surprised when he meets a colossal Whale? But the sea is teeming with them and they will team up with Mouse to help him on his way.

THINGS YOU'LL NEED

- **Old pants or ½ yard (0.5m) dark fabric**
- **White fabric:** ¼ yard or fat quarter
- **Polyfill**
- **2 small buttons**

What am I doing here? Showing you my laundry? Geez, I thought we were making a Whale for Mouse's South Pole adventure! We are. We are. This isn't my *laundry*—this is a pile we could use to make a Whale. I discovered

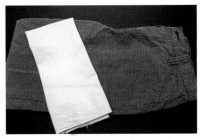

that it only takes one pant leg to make a Whale, and some pants are really perfect for it. You can use an old pair of jeans or Dockers. You don't have to, though. You can also just use regular fabric. But if you do want to use a pair of pants, make sure you ask permission first. Don't cut up a family member's jeans unless they okay it. You also need some white fabric.

1. Here I go, cutting off a leg of my pants. Wheeeee!

2. You are really going to need to use the patterns (on pullout page P2) on this baby. No free cutting here, let me tell you. Whale is made from some pretty bizarre shapes. I'll be cutting 3 of the shapes from my pants—the upper body (2 pieces), the flippers (4 pieces), and the tail (2 pieces).

3. I'm using a thick Sharpie to mark the patterns on my pants. The pants are thick, so the Sharpie won't bleed through.

4. Here's what everything should look like so far. After you mark your patterns, you can cut the pieces out. Cut about ¼" (0.6cm) outside your line.

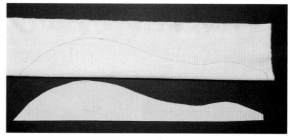

5. Use the white fabric for Whale's underbelly. Mark this piece on the fold.

6. It'll look like this.

7. After you cut it out and unfold it, it'll look like this:

8. Whale also has 2 really long, weirdly shaped white side pieces.

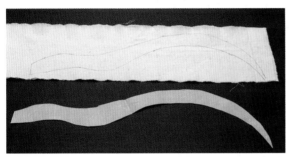

9. Here's what they look like when you've cut them out.

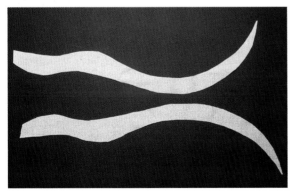

10. To make the sides of Whale, you're going to sew the top portion to the white bottom portion, right sides together. The pieces will fit together like this.

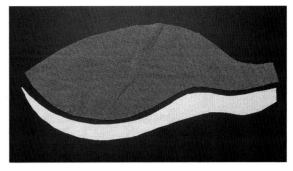

11. This isn't going to be a comfortable fit because of all the curves, so you need to sew very slowly on the line you drew and pull the fabric together to make it align. This is that technique I showed you in Curve Madness (page 12). Just sew slowly and try not to think evil thoughts. It's going to buckle, but don't let that disturb you.

12. When you open it up, crease the seam with your nail to get it to lie flat. You can also iron it flat. Get help using the iron if you aren't used to using it—irons can be more deadly than hot glue guns.

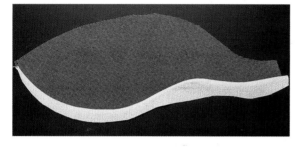

13. Repeat this process so that you have both side pieces sewn.

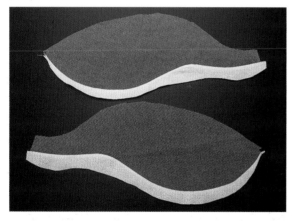

14. Next, place the pieces right sides together and stitch across Whale's back. Start at the nose and work your way back.

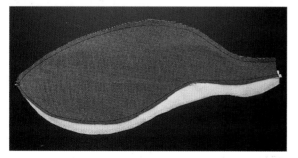

15. Go ahead and attach the underbelly. Start with a single side; then sew the other side. Remember to leave a gap. This time, leave a large gap—big enough for you to put your whole hand through. You'll need the extra room to maneuver when you stuff this big guy.

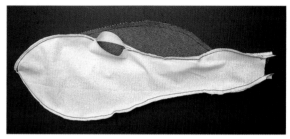

16. Now find the tail pieces. With right sides together, stitch together the tail, leaving the flat end open. Do that little *snippy-snip-snip* thing around the curved parts of the tail to help it lie flat when you turn it. But don't turn it yet!

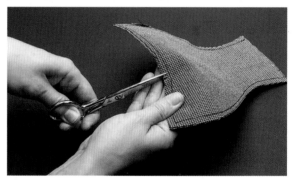

17. Now line up the tail with the back end of Whale. You can sew the tail on by machine, but honestly, I sewed mine on by hand. It's narrow, and I had better control with the hand sewing.

18. After the tail is sewed on, turn your mighty Whale!

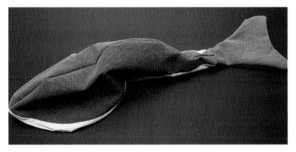

19. Now *stuff, stuff, stuff.* Lots of stuffing. Take your time. Pack the polyfill pretty tightly. Use a matching thread to stitch up the gap you left open.

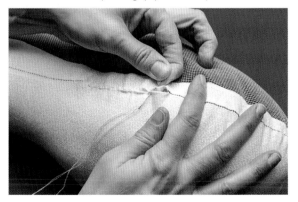

20. Now reach for the flippers. With right sides together, stitch a pair of flippers. Be sure to leave the flat side open.

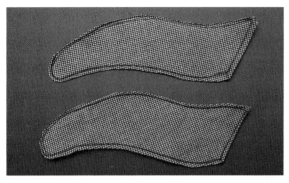

21. Turn the flippers. You might want to iron them flat.

22. Attach a flipper to each side of Whale using a matching thread. Tuck under the raw edges and use a slipstitch. Check the pattern and photo for positioning.

23. Whale eyes are typically small. I'm going to use these neat buttons.

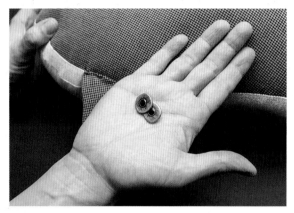

24. After you sew the eyes in place, Whale is ready to roam the seas.

This Is Mouse—An Adventure in Sewing

Mouse Goes to the South Pole

Mouse's next stop is the South Pole! He'll need a sturdy sled and a team of sled dogs to help him get around.

Rabbits aren't built for this kind of weather, though. They soon get tired. They ask Mouse if they can ride on the sled while he pulls. Mouse isn't too keen on this idea.

The Rabbits get stubborn and burrow in. They've had enough of sled pulling.

Mouse must move on. It's cold and lonely here.

Mouse is getting very, very cold. He finds an igloo and squeezes in. But he forgets to tuck in his tail! In the morning, a Penguin sees his frozen tail peeking out of the igloo. He runs to tell his brothers what he has seen.

The bravest brother approaches the igloo. "Come out with your hands up!" he shouts. "It's only me," says Mouse.

The Penguins are fascinated by this hairy little animal. He keeps complaining that he is cold, but he has a lot of fur.

"Penguins don't have fur. If we get really, really cold, we just huddle together."

Mouse's tummy starts rumbling. The Penguins tell him that they eat Fish, but that doesn't sound too good to him. He leaves the Penguins to search for other food but can't find much on his own. Then he meets a Seal.

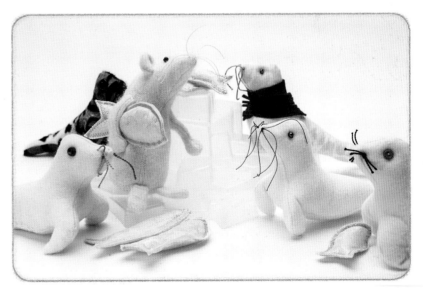

The Seal and his friends teach Mouse how to fish. Mouse is good at catching Fish, but he doesn't want to eat them. He just gives them to the Seals. Mouse still feels hungry as he wanders off.

Mouse has an odd feeling as he trudges along the ice. Is someone watching him?

Why, yes! Someone is! It's a huge Whale.

"I think you are lost, little Mouse," says the Whale. "Climb on my back, and I will show you the ocean before I take you to land again."

Mouse has a fantastic ride, swimming with Whales—a glorious end to his chilly adventure.

Blast Off

If Mouse thought the South Pole was cold, he's not going to find much comfort in outer space! Still, he's determined to go where no Mouse has gone before.

Space Gear

RAY GUN

You can't send Mouse off on a potentially dangerous mission in space without some sort of protection, so you're going to arm him with a ray gun. This is an essentially useless weapon. The only thing it can do is make objects float. But it might come in handy, just the same. I, for one, am always looking for a good use for dental floss. I want to use it on anything that does not have to do with actually flossing my teeth. I do know that The Flossing of Teeth is vitally important, mind you. I just don't like to do it.

THINGS YOU'LL NEED

- **1 disposable flosser**
- **Ribbon or cording:** about 4" (10cm)
- **1 coned bead**
- **Hot glue gun**

1. So today you have the opportunity to repurpose one of those vile disposable flossers and convert it into something more useful: a ray gun!

2. Use a black Sharpie marker to make the flosser black.

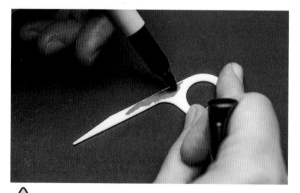

3. Now hunt up a bit of thin ribbon or cording. I'm using red cording here. You also need some sort of coned bead.

4. Slip an end of the cording through the coned bead and tie a knot in the other end.

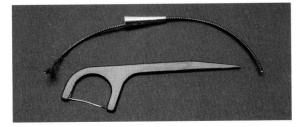

5. Pull the knotted end of the cording into the bead. Fire up that glue gun (mind your fingers!) and glue the end of the coned bead to the tip of the flosser.

Voilà! Instant ray gun! Mouse is ready for action!

HELMET

THINGS YOU'LL NEED
- **Egg carton**
- **Aluminum foil**
- **Clear tape**

Every space traveler needs a helmet, and Mouse is no exception! Never mind the fact that this particular helmet will do nothing to protect him from the elements on another planet. It just looks cool.

1. You can make a helmet for Mouse using an egg carton.

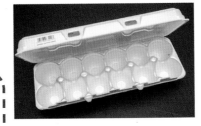

2. Cut a single egg holder out of the carton.

3. Trim away the excess so that only the bowl part remains.

4. Cover the helmet with a small piece of aluminum foil.

5. You can try it on Mouse to see how it fits so far.

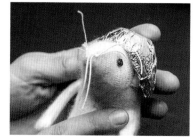

7. To hold the helmet in place, you can tape the ends inside the helmet.

6. Make a strap from aluminum foil. Cut a piece about 1" × 7" (2.5cm × 17.8cm) and fold it to fit under Mouse's chin.

ROCKET

Mouse needs a rocket to travel into space. Let's make him one using a brightly colored cotton, such as red or blue, and white cotton.

THINGS YOU'LL NEED

- **Brightly colored cotton:** ½ yard (0.5m)
- **White cotton:** ½ yard (0.5m)
- **Batting:** ½ yard (0.5m)
- **Cardboard (poster board or cardboard from a cereal box):** 3 pieces 8" × 15" (20.3cm × 38.1cm)
- **Clear plastic for window**
- **Gold cording:** enough to go around plastic window
- **Hot glue gun**

This Is Mouse—An Adventure in Sewing

You also need quilt batting and some pieces of cardboard.

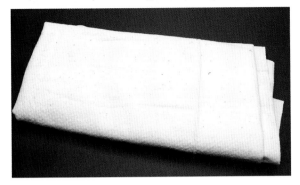

Plus the rocket pattern (on pullout page P2).

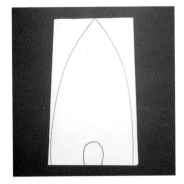

- -

1. This rocket has 3 faces and each face is made with several layers. Trace the pattern onto pieces of cardboard 3 times and cut them out. When you make the rocket, these pieces of cardboard are actually going to be imbedded into the rocket to give it support.

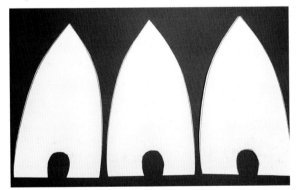

2. Cut out 3 rockets from the white fabric.

3. And 3 rockets from the quilt batting.

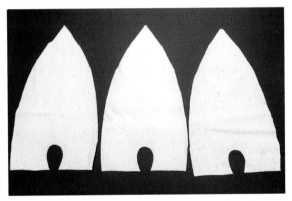

4. And 3 more rockets from the brightly colored fabric.

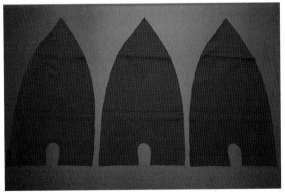

5. For each side of the rocket, you need a brightly colored layer, a cardboard layer, a batting layer, and a white layer, in that order. Stack up the layers for a side of the rocket. The right sides of the brightly colored layer and the white layer should be facing out.

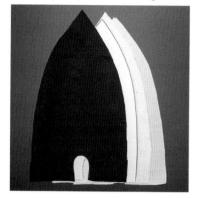

6. Using a tight zigzag stitch in matching thread, sew together all the layers all the way around the edges. Do this for 2 of the rocket sides.

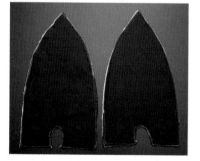

7. The third side gets a large window. Hunt up a piece of clear plastic. I'm using a bubble of plastic that was packaging on a toy. You can find this sort of thing on a lot of packaging. It doesn't have to be round. Mine is about 3" (7.6cm) wide.

8. To make the window fit, center and trace around your shape. Then cut a hole through all 3 fabric layers as well as the cardboard layer.

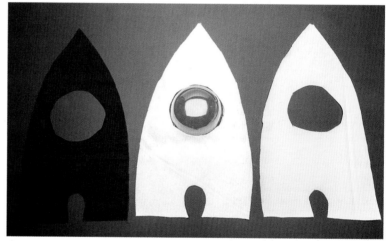

9. As with the other sides, you need to sew together the layers of the rocket with a tight zigzag stitch around the edges. Before you sew the outside edges, though, sew around the window first. Just go really, really slowly.

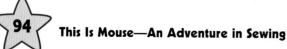

10. Now, if you're like me, and I really do hope you are not, you'll have made a mess of things sewing around this window. My stitches are all kind of crazy around that window. While I hang my head in shame, though, I'll also be reaching for some gold cording.

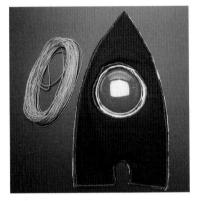

11. If you are not a hot mess like I am, and if your window looks perfect, you can skip this step. But I tell you: a world of hurt can be hidden with this gold cording. It was worth burning my fingers with the hot glue gun to tack it down. I braided my cording before I glued it down.

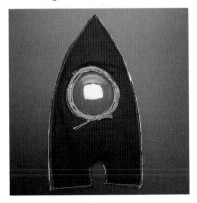

12. Start sewing the rocket's sides now. Take the 2 windowless panels and zigzag the heck out of them. Oh, wait, that's not very helpful, is it? What I mean to say is, sew together 2 of the edges with a tight zigzag. Go slowly because you have that cardboard in there too—remember?

13. Here's a view of it from the inside:

14. Now repeat the same procedure to add the final, windowed panel. Go slow. No prize for being the first to finish.

15. Check pattern pullout page P2 for a triangular piece. Cut this out of cardboard. It's the piece that you insert into the rocket to give Mouse something to stand on. Stand Mouse on this triangle and then slide it up into the rocket until he's looking out the window.

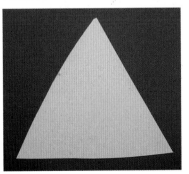

16. Before it launches—and this is optional—you can add a little flourish to the top of the rocket. I used a fancy pin-sort-of-thing I found at a craft store.

Mouse is ready for liftoff!

FLYING SAUCER

You can bet that there will be Aliens on this other planet that Mouse is going to, and they'll need a flying saucer to get around. You can make a really simply one using pie tins. It won't take but a minute.

THINGS YOU'LL NEED
- **2 disposable pie tins:** 5" (12.7cm) diameter
- **Hot glue gun**
- **Beads, flat marbles, LEDs (*optional*)**

1. Cut a small, round hatch in the top of a tin. Ask for help if you're using a really sharp knife like mine.

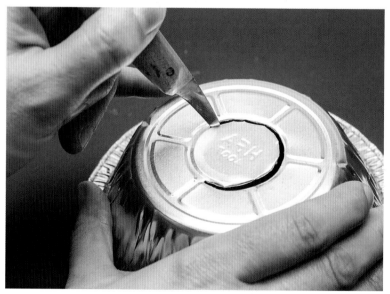

2. Don't cut all the way around your hatch or it will become detached. Leave a small section uncut so you can prop open the hatch and close it after the Aliens are inside. Careful: the cut edges may be sharp!

3. Use a hot glue gun to glue the bottom pie tin to the top tin. Mind your fingers, though—that glue gun gets hot!

4. Your ship is all ready for its Alien pilot!

5. If you want to make a fancier ship, you can embellish the ship with beads, flat marbles, LEDs, or anything else that looks good to you.

ROCK CAVE

The Aliens that Mouse will meet live on a rocky planet. They build their homes from the rocks they find. We, however, will use Styrofoam for building.

THINGS YOU'LL NEED
- **Styrofoam balls and cones:** an assortment
- **Hot glue gun**
- **Paint**

1. I've selected an assortment of foam balls and cones we can choose from.

2. The largest ball is 8″ (20cm) in diameter.

3. Slice off a section of the ball to make a flat bottom.

4. Mark an opening in the ball with a Sharpie.

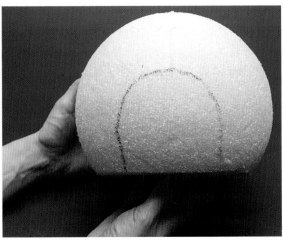

5. I used a combination of weapons to hollow out the ball—my husband's favorite bagel knife and one of my dad's carving knives. Shhhh…don't tell! You'll probably want to get help with this step. Do be careful—knives can be sharp.

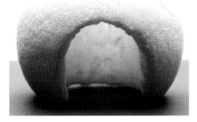

6. I'll flip mine over so you can see what it looks like underneath.

7. After you have the main chamber hollowed out, add other embellishments to your rock cave. I hollowed out a smaller 6" (15cm) ball, sliced off the

bottom, and attached it to the side of the main chamber using my hot glue gun. (Yes, I burned my fingers. Ouch!) I also added smaller balls to the top and a few cool cones to the side and bottom. You can come up with all sorts of neat combinations.

8. To make the rock cave look rock-like, you can use a special type of paint. It's called American Accents stone paint (by Rust-Oleum), and you can get it at the hardware store.

Be sure to follow the directions and only use spray paint outdoors or in an open garage. Oh, and put down lots of newspapers to catch the overspray. You might want to test your spray paint, as some kinds can sort of melt the Styrofoam if they are sprayed from too close. Now, if that's the effect you want on your cave, go for it! But if you don't, experiment with spraying with the can about 12"–18" (30cm–46cm) from the Styrofoam. You can also paint the Styrofoam with water-based craft paints.

9. After spraying the cave, let it dry before you populate it with Aliens!

Robot

Finished size: about 3″ (8cm) tall

Mouse will need some technical help getting his rocket ready for takeoff. Let's build him a few Robots to do the work. We'll make them out of polymer clay.

THINGS YOU'LL NEED

- **Polymer clay**
- **Pasta maker (*optional*)**
- **Aluminum foil**
- **Screws, beads, springs, and gears (for eyes, arms, etc.)**

There are several brands of clay you can use—Premo! Sculpey or Fimo, for example—whatever you have on hand or can find easily at a craft or hobby store.

1. You need 2 blocks of clay. I'm making my Robot out of copper clay to give it that metallic feel. You can choose any color you like, though.

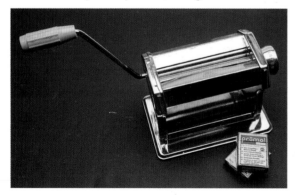

I also like to use a pasta maker to help soften the clay, but you can also just warm the clay up by holding it. For. A. Long. Time. Until it gets soft. If I don't use the pasta thingie, I usually find a Loved One to hold and warm up my clay… "Here—hold this…" (And then I run away for a while.)

2. To warm up the clay, it sometimes helps to break it into smaller pieces.

3. If you are using a pasta thingie, line the pieces on the top of the press.

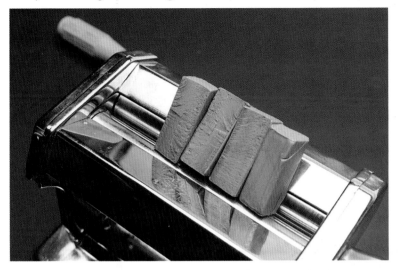

4. Crank away! Pass the clay through the press several times to get it soft enough to work with.

5. In the end, you want 2 soft balls of clay.

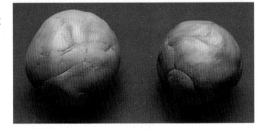

6. Shape these into 2 flat-sided objects—a small cube for Robot's head and a longer rectangle for its body.

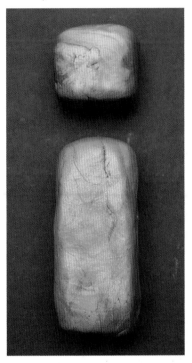

7. Press the 2 pieces together to connect them and put them on an aluminum foil–lined baking sheet. The clay will have to cook in the oven in order to harden. But wait! Don't put anything in the oven yet!

8. Now you need to figure out what you want your Robot to look like. It needs arms and legs and embellishments for its chest. Here's an assortment of weird things I found in our garage. Remember to pick things that won't melt when you bake Robot in the oven later!

9. For my Robot, I'm using 2 screws for the legs. I just inserted them into the clay at the bottom of the long rectangle.

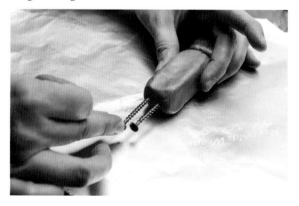

10. Then I took these unusual wire beads and stretched them out a bit to make them look like arms.

11. Arms inserted! Check!

12. Eyes next, and weird little metal horns on Robot's head—they're made from silver cone beads. Mouth is optional.

13. I always think of Robots as having clockworks in them, so I pressed a few metal gears into its chest to suggest that.

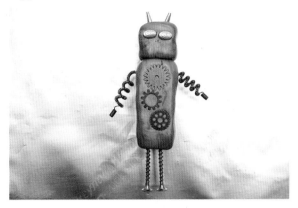

14. Bake the Robot. Be sure to follow the instructions on your clay package to see how long and at what temperature the clay needs to bake.

Each Robot you make can look different, depending on what color of clay you use and what sorts of embellishments you decorate it with.

Alien

You'll soon see that the planet Mouse lands on is heavily populated with colorful little Aliens.

Use a pair of toddler-size socks for each Alien you want to make.

1. Turn the first sock inside out and lay it flat.

THINGS YOU'LL NEED

- **1 pair toddler-size socks**
- **Polyfill**
- **Felt scraps**
- **Hot glue gun**

3. You should also draw a pair of stubby little legs.

2. Using a marking pen, or in my case just a black Sharpie, draw an Alien head on the top of the sock. The heel of the sock is going to be Alien's nose. So you need to draw the 2 antennae that poke out from the top of its head. They have little round balls on the tops.

4. Now slowly stitch along the lines you've drawn. Take your time, especially around the antennae. They are narrow.

5. Trim away any excess sock.

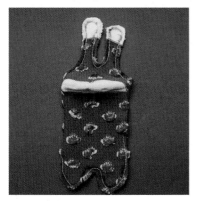

6. Poke the blade of your scissors into its side (no, it won't hurt it), just enough to make a small cut so you can turn it. I say "it" here because it's very hard to determine an Alien's gender just by glancing at it. You really need to spend time with them and get to know them better before you can tell for sure.

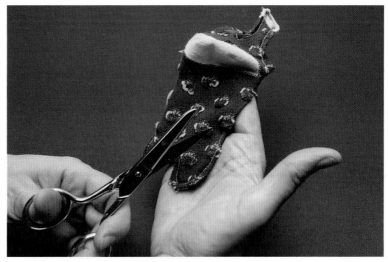

7. Give Alien a little flip to turn it right side out.

8. Go back to the second sock now. Cut off the toe part, just up from the heel.

9. Turn this little sock nib inside out and free sew a pair of short, stubby Alien arms.

10. Trim away any excess sockage and gently turn its arms. Turn, not twist. Twisting arms is another matter altogether and simply not warranted here.

11. Here's a look at all the Alien parts now.

12. Put a little polyfill into Alien's body; you won't need much. Then use a matching thread to stitch up the gap.

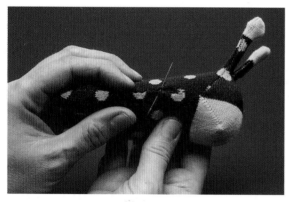

13. While you're stitching away, you might as well attach both arms. One to each side of its body, please. Although I suppose you could put the arms anywhere you like. It *is* an Alien. Remember to tuck under your raw edges and use a matching thread and slipstitch to hide your work.

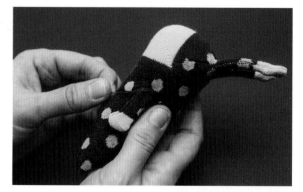

14. Hmmm ... how about some eyes? Maybe 2 tiny felt circles?

15. Attach the eyes using a hot glue gun. Mind those fingers!
You know what happens to me.

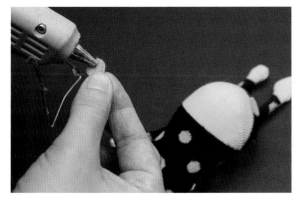

Make as many Aliens as you need.

⭐ Mouse Goes to Outer Space ⭐

Before Mouse can go on his mission, he needs a rocket. Who better to advise him than the Chief Robot of Rocketry? Mouse learns that work is already under way on his rocket.

He just needs to decide which one to take—red or blue? Red, definitely!

Blasting off is noisy and bumpy. Mouse feels a little carsick. Or rocketsick. But that soon goes away as he gazes out his window and looks into space.

After traveling many, many, many miles, Mouse lands on a mysterious Earth-like planet. He puts on his helmet, ray gun at the ready. Immediately, he is met by Alien life.

No need for the ray gun, Mouse! These Aliens are friendly.

The Alien landing party introduces itself. There's Derek, Chester, and Corkscrew.

Back at the Aliens' rocky home, the lookout is quick to spot the returning landing party. A Hairy Creature is traveling among them.

Some Aliens are afraid of Hairy Creature, so they hide.

But it doesn't take long for Mouse to put everyone at ease.

Soon, the Aliens love him. They want to make him an honorary member of their clan. But Mouse is getting homesick, so he makes his good-byes.

"We will miss the Hairy One," the Aliens say. And they mean it.

Mouse will miss the Aliens, too. Especially their curious way of speaking without having mouths.

Thanks for coming with Mouse on his adventures. You are excellent company. Will you do it again?

Join Mouse in his next set of adventures—but before he heads out again, Mouse is heading home for a much-needed rest!

About the Author

Brenna Maloney is the author of *Socks Appeal*, *Sockology*, and *Sock It To Me*. She lives and works in Washington, D.C., with her husband and two sons. Follow Brenna on brennamaloney.com.

Other books by Brenna:

Bloopers

"I told you this was a bad idea. Does anyone see any ice?

"Norbert! You come down from there this instant!"

"I appreciate your optimism, but I still don't think I'll fit."

"I can give you a good price on this igloo—cheap!"